# THE Grizzard SAMPLER

# THE Grizzard SAMPLER

A Collection of the
Early Writings of Lewis Grizzard

Ç₽
PUBLISHED BY
Peachtree Publishers, Ltd.
494 Armour Circle NE
Atlanta, Georgia 30324

The material found in this collection was previously published by
Peachtree Publishers, Ltd., under the following titles: *Kathy Sue
Loudermilk, I Love You: A Good Beer Joint is Hard to Find and Other
Facts of Life*, 1979; *Won't You Come Home, Billy Bob Bailey?*, 1980;
*Don't Sit Under the Grits Tree with Anyone Else But Me*, 1981; *They
Tore Out My Heart and Stomped That Sucker Flat*, 1982; *If Love Were
Oil, I'd Be About a Quart Low: Lewis Grizzard on Women*, 1983; *Elvis Is
Dead and I Don't Feel So Good Myself*, 1984; *Shoot Low, Boys—They're
Ridin' Shetland Ponies*, 1985. All titles copyright Lewis Grizzard.

Quotations used in introduction reprinted with special permission
of King Features Syndicate.

Book and cover design by Terri Fox
Additional text by Stephanie Thomas

10 9 8 7 6 5 4 3 2 1

Manufactured in the United States of America

Library of Congress Cataloging-in-Publication Data:
Grizzard, Lewis, 1946–1994
     [Selections. 1994]
     The Grizzard sampler : the best of the early writings of
Lewis grizzard / Lewis Grizzard.
          p. cm.
     ISBN 1-56145-099-5
     I. Title.
PN6162.G7825   1994                          94-33028
814′ .54—dc20                                      CIP

# Publisher's Note

Lewis McDonald Grizzard, Jr., was born on October 20, 1946 at Fort Benning, Georgia. He spent most of his childhood in Moreland, Georgia, a town immortalized in many of his books. Grizzard began his career as a writer with newspapers while a student at the University of Georgia. He left the university one course short of graduation to work for the *Atlanta Journal* in 1967. (He later completed the course by correspondence and received his degree in 1984.)

His career as a book author began in 1978 when he brought a brown paper grocery bag filled with his columns to Helen Elliott, founder of the then newly formed Peachtree Publishers. These columns became the basis for his first book (one of seven with Peachtree) called *Kathy Sue Loudermilk, I Love You*, which was published in September 1979.

Helen Elliott delighted Grizzard by delivering the first advance copy of his new book—just received from the printer—to him on the tennis courts of the Bitsy Grant Tennis Center in the same brown bag he had used to carry his would-be manuscript to her a year earlier. Thus began a close personal and professional friendship that intertwined the destinies of the fledgling publisher and author.

This ritual continued for each of the books that Grizzard published while Helen Elliott was alive. After her death from cancer in January of 1983, the grocery bag was retired to the archives of Peachtree Publishers.

In a moving column marking Elliott's death, Grizzard described his publisher as "his link to God." He said of her: "She prayed me through a thousand nights in front of a stubborn typewriter that just sat there and stared back at me as if to say, 'who are you kidding?'"

Grizzard's relationship with Peachtree remained strong even after the death of his friend and patron. His popularity increased with every book, while his syndicated newspaper column gained ever wider audiences, peaking at a syndication of 450 papers. His final two books with Peachtree both made the much coveted *New York Times* Best Seller List and catapulted Grizzard and Peachtree to national recognition. In 1986, Grizzard accepted an offer for a multi-book contract from Villard, a division of Random House, where he published another seven books.

Lewis Grizzard died in March 20, 1994 from complications caused by a heart condition.

While their paths diverged, Peachtree and Grizzard remain linked by their shared history. We have chosen to honor his memory by publishing *The Grizzard Sampler*, drawn from among our favorite stories from his Peachtree books, all of which are still in print at this writing. We hope that whether a newcomer to his unique style or an already loyal fan, you will enjoy this special tribute to one of the South's most identifiable voices.

This collection of the early writings of
Lewis Grizzard
is dedicated in his memory
to the journalism students
of the University of Georgia.

*Dedra Grizzard, October 1994*

A portion of the proceeds from the sale of this book
will be contributed to
The Lewis Grizzard Scholarship Fund
Henry W. Grady College of Journalism & Mass Communication
The University of Georgia
Athens Georgia 30602-3018

For information about this scholarship fund, direct correspondence to the attention of
Dean J. Thomas Russell.

# Contents

"So this is what's happened to the South since William Faulkner left."

*Randy Harvey,* Chicago Sun-Times

In *1979, Jimmy Carter was president, the Camp David peace talks were underway, and Iran was in the news. And Lewis Grizzard was a newspaper columnist whose bag of clippings had just been turned into his very first book,* Kathy Sue Loudermilk, I Love You: A Good Beer Joint is Hard to Find and other Facts of Life. *This book gathered together the best of his newspaper columns and introduced him to a larger audience, an audience who couldn't get enough of his down-to-earth and very southern humor. In fact, the first printing of* Kathy Sue Loudermilk *sold out in the first week it was available.*

Kathy Sue
Loudermilk,
I Love
You

A
Good
Beer Joint is
Hard to Find
and
other
Facts of
Life
by
Lewis
Grizzard

1979

# • Cold Beer and Country Music

I fell in love with country music when I was nine years old and somebody slipped a nickel into the juke box at Steve Smith's truck stop in my hometown of Moreland, Georgia, and played a hurtin' song by Hank Williams. Everybody likes beer, of course.

# The Den Mother of Country Music

NASHVILLE • They put Tootsie Bess to rest on a snowy hillside in Nashville Tuesday afternoon. When she died of cancer at sixty-four the other day, they should have lowered every flag in the city to half-mast. She was somebody. She was the den mother of country music.

Without her, there might not have been the stardom and the music of people like Tom T. Hall. Or Kris Kristofferson. Or Roger Miller. Or Johnny Rodrigues. Or Hank Williams, or any number of pickers and singers who have made what otherwise would have been nothing more than Chattanooga North into a multi-million dollar recording Mecca called Music City U.S.A.

Without her, many who stayed and finally caught their dreams might have long since caught the next bus back home. Like a maid said at Tootsie's funeral Tuesday, "You can find rhinestones and applause in Nashville, but before you do, it can be the loneliest place in the world."

Hattie Louise "Tootsie" Bess ran a beer joint in Nashville at Fifth and Broadway called Tootsie's Orchid Lounge. There was a back door. It led to an alley that led to the stage entrance of the old Ryman Auditorium, for years the home of the Grand Ole Opry.

Grant Turner, the Opry announcer, said, "You could leave Tootsie's at 7:58 and still be on stage at the Opry at eight o'clock." So many did just that.

When Tom T. Hall first came to Nashville, he nearly starved. Tootsie fed him. Tootsie encouraged him. Tootsie gave him pocket money. Today, Tom T. Hall sells millions of records and trucks on television.

Kris Kristofferson worked construction and swept floors in Nashville while trying to peddle his music. He was one of Tootsie's pets. She kept him going until another star was born.

Roger Miller was a Nashville bellhop. He would write one of his biggest hits, "Dang Me," in a booth at Tootsie's.

"She ran a beer joint," said Tom T. Hall, "but to young songwriters and musicians, she was a small finance company, a booking agent, and a counselor."

Maybe Ernest Tubb put it even better: "Tootsie," he said, "was the softest touch in town."

I was in her place only once. But I remember the beer being cold and the atmosphere being warm and Tootsie saying as my party left, "Y'all come back when you can stay longer."

Her juke box had million sellers. It also had non-sellers. When nobody else would play a youngster's record, Tootsie would put it next to "Hello Walls," and give the kid the best chance she could.

She kept order with a hatpin. Get rowdy and out you went at the point of her hatpin. Come back tomorrow and apologize, and all was forgiven.

There were five inches of fresh snow on the ground in Nashville Tuesday. Still, the funeral home was packed with people and flowers.

The registry was a country music who's who. Mel Tillis sent flowers. There was a wreath from Ben Smathers and his mountain cloggers. Ernest Tubb and his son Justin sent a heart-shaped arrangement. There was a break in the middle of the heart. It was pierced with a hatpin.

Roy Acuff sat down front for the services. One of the Wilburn Brothers was close to him. Included in the grieving family was Tootsie's son-in-law, who is an Opry drummer. Tom T. Hall was one of the pallbearers. Grant Turner got up and said a few words. And Connie Smith stood behind Tootsie's lavender casket and sang "In the Sweet By and By," "Amazing Grace," and "How Great Thou Art." She has never sounded better.

Tootsie had friends who weren't stars. "She was just as happy to see a ditch-digger walk in as the biggest name in town," said a friend. Sitting next to a millionaire singer at the funeral was a man in a service station outfit. He hadn't had time to wash the grease off his hands.

The preacher read a telegram from Tennessee Senator Howard Baker. He talked about the necessity of loving one another and said Mrs. Bess, as he called her, performed that task exactly as the Good Book intended.

It could be the Good Lord likes the company of a bighearted saloon-keeper too.

# Willie at the White House

WASHINGTON • People wearing bags over their heads and carrying signs that screamed about "massacres" in their native Iran paraded in front of the White House Wednesday evening.

To the north of the city at Camp David, three powerful leaders of three powerful nations struggled to find a way to bring peace to another troubled land.

The papers were filled with stories of death and destruction in Nicaragua, and half the world was on strike.

But the night was clear and cool, and the moon was full and bright in Washington Wednesday. And out on the south lawn of the White House, a million miles from everything else, a bearded man wearing a red bandanna took a long pull from a wine bottle and commenced to sing.

He sang "Whiskey River" first; then he sang "Crazy" and "Amazing Grace" and "Georgia" and something called "Blue Eyes Crying in the Rain." As he sang "Blue Eyes Crying in the Rain" I had a thought, probably an outrageous one, but at least worth a moment of consideration:

Jimmy Carter didn't make his own party Wednesday night, the one he threw to honor stockcar drivers. His wife announced to the crowd that "only something the magnitude of the summit talks would have kept him away."

He made a mistake by not coming. And he made a mistake by not bringing Egypt's Sadat and Israel's Begin with him.

Sit the two of them down together in front of Willie Nelson, I thought. Bring the people with the bags over their heads inside, too. Give them all a cold beer and let them listen to Willie Nelson. After "Blue Eyes Crying in the Rain," who would still want to fight?

Wednesday night was Jimmy Carter fulfilling a promise. When he was governor of Georgia, he made it an annual practice to host stockcar drivers and even sportswriters at the mansion on West Paces Ferry.

You know about stockcar racing. Stockcar racing isn't Watkins Glen or spiffy gentlemen in sleek Porsches and Ferraris. It is Talledega

7

and Daytona and Atlanta International Raceway and beer and fried chicken and a punch in the nose because you said a Chevrolet can whip a Dodge or, worse, you insulted the glorious memory of Fireball Roberts.

"Jimmy told us if he ever got to be president," explained driver David Pearson, "we would share in some of the glory. Here we are."

And there they were. Pearson, Petty, Waldrip, Yarborough, and Bill France, the head kabolla of stockcar racing. And even some sportswriters and even Billy Carter, and especially Willie Nelson, who sang with Amy and Rosalynn and Billy's wife, Sybil.

The night was heavy with double-knit and denim.

The Washington papers the next day didn't quite know what to make of the affair. They said it did prove we are under the reign of a populist president. They went into great detail concerning the Carters' love for stockcar racing and explained stockcar racing grew in the South from an earlier preoccupation with running moonshine.

"I ain't never run moonshine," Richard Petty told a reporter. "But I don't know about the rest of my family."

I go back to those parties at the governor's mansion. The first one was a flop because Rosalynn had charge of the food and entertainment. She offered an exotic menu that included fishlike things that still had their eyes. The entertainment was an operatic trio.

I can still see A. J. Foyt shifting uncomfortably from one cowboy boot to another and Jabe Thomas driving to the front of the mansion in his mechanic's truck. I can still hear somebody saying, "This would make Curtis Turner roll over in his grave." Rosalynn Carter stepped onto the bandshell behind the White House Wednesday night and apologized for all that. She had learned her lesson. The fare this evening was beer and wine and roast beef and ham and corn bread. The program announced. "Selections by Willie Nelson."

I could probably dabble around in all this for some hidden political meaning. But the heck with that.

What happened Wednesday night at the home of the president of the United States was a large group mostly Southern people got together in the backyard for a picinic and to listen to one of their own sing his red bandanna off. Andy Jackson used to give the same kind of parties here, and he wound up on the twenty dollar bill.

In the middle of that singing, when people had squared off to clog on the lawn, a fellow I know from Georgia came to my table and whispered in my ear:

"My great-grandfather was wounded at the Battle of Sharpsburg. He was captured at Gettysburg. He had to limp all the way home to Georgia. If he could see this tonight, he'd think we won after all."

# •The View From Left Field

I knew it was time for me to get out of sportswriting when I covered the 1978 Super Bowl game between Dallas and Denver and enjoyed the halftime show that featured dogs catching frisbees more than I did the football game. I will still fall into a sports column now and then, however. It's comfortable there, like an old pair of sneakers.

# At the Ball Game With My Dad

I would have taken my father out to the ball game Tuesday night. I would have taken him to the Atlanta Stadium to see Pete Rose try to break Wee Willie Keeler's hitting streak record.

His birthday is Saturday. He would have been sixty-six. A trip to the ball game would have been a nice present from a son to his father.

He was an athlete himself, my dad. And he was a strapping man with alleged blinding speed in his youth. He was taller than Pete Rose, but similar in stocky frame. One time he picked up the back of a 1949 Hudson. I saw him do it.

My father would have loved Tuesday night at the ball park. Nice summer evening. Big, noisy crowd. My father always enjoyed singing the national anthem at baseball games.

He had a big voice, a booming voice that could cut you down at one hundred yards when it broke into "He Leadeth Me" or our national anthem, his two favorite songs. He always sang along when they played the national anthem, no matter where or what event. One time I said to him, "I wish you wouldn't sing so loud. It's embarrassing."

He said to me, "Son, it's embarrassing when you don't sing along with me."

Tuesday night, just before Pete Rose stepped up to bat, going for forty-five straight, my father and I would have stood shoulder-to-shoulder and sung the national anthem together.

Pete Rose is my father's kind of man, I was thinking when Rose approached the plate in the first inning. Just before the game began, he had his picture made with a crippled boy and put his hat on the crippled boy's head.

"Look at the way that man moves," my father would have said of Rose. "He doesn't waste a motion. He has speed. He has strength. He has determination. That's the kind of man you want in a foxhole with you."

My father was a soldier. A damn good one.

His only objection to Pete Rose might have been Rose's hair. I noticed it precariously near his shoulders. His ears disappeared weeks ago. My father wore a crew cut. He thought everybody else should.

"I'll never get used to long hair on a ballplayer or a soldier," he might have said as Larry McWilliams of the Braves threw the first pitch of the ball game—a curve—"It's not what the Lord intended."

The curve to Rose is low for ball one. And then a foul deep to right that misses being a double by five feet. A fast ball outside, a curve catches the inside corner, the count goes full, two more fouls, then ball four. The streak holds at forty-four.

I never saw a major league baseball game with my father. We saw plenty of service ball together. He once coached the Fort Benning team. Coached in a Hawaiian shirt and a straw hat.

Later, we bummed around south Georgia one summer. My father had fallen on hard times, but he kept a ten-year-old fed and cared for during three of the best months of my life.

That summer, we spent night after hot south Georgia night fighting gnats and eating peanuts in broken-down Class D parks in Waycross and Moultire and Tifton where something called the Georgia-Florida league still had life.

There is something special about a man with his son at a baseball game. A man and his son sat next to me Monday night when Pete Rose extended his batting streak to forty-four. As Pete strode to the plate for the first time, the boy asked his dad if he would take him to the rest room.

"Not now, son," said the father. "Not now. Pete Rose is batting."

The boy held on, uncomfortably, but appearing to understand the necessity of the effort.

When a man takes his son to a basketball game, I think, if establishes a link, one that won't easily be broken even in the face of a subsequent premature parting that might leave other scars.

I know that to be a fact.

Rose came up for a second time. "Let's go, Pete," my father would have screamed, loud enough to be heard in LaGrange. What the heck. Let him have his fun.

First pitch, Rose swings. A shot up the middle. Young McWilliams' gloved hand appears from nowhere and spears the drive. Rose drops his bat and gives the youngster a hand. Mostly, my father would have enjoyed the game Tuesday night because it was a vivid American scene. It was an act of patriotism, somehow, to have been there.

He would have looked at his fellow Americans eating hot dogs and drinking beer, he would have heard their cheers for the home runs by Horner and Murphy, and he would have said something like, "This is why your daddy went to war, son. This is what we fought to keep."

Rose is up again. The inning is the fifth. The game is tied, 3–3. A fake bunt, ball one. Another ball. Then a ground out to short. The tension builds.

Now, it is the seventh. The brutal Gene Garber is pitching for the Braves. A runner is on. One out. A fast ball strike on the outside corner. Two straight balls. A foul tip, the count is even. Then, another shot by Rose, toward left, the opposite field. But Horner is there for the out and a double play.

A final chance, and only that, remains. The ninth. The game has turned to slaughter. The Reds, for once, are the victims, 16–4. Atlanta has twenty-one hits. Even Garber has one. Pete Rose, whose name even sounds like a line drive, has none.

Two outs. Rose at bat. "Pete! Pete! Pete!" the stadium is begging.

The first pitch from Garber. An attempted drag bunt to third goes foul. Two straight balls. A foul tip.

The ball leaves Garber's hand. A split second later, we will know.

Strike three. Swinging. It is over.

What Pete Rose did—hit safely in forty-four straight games—wasn't a man on the moon, I reminded myself as the stadium lights dimmed. It wasn't a lonely flight across the Atlantic or the first heart transplant.

But it was a good and honorable thing, a fierce man with a bat in his hand, playing a boy's game as it was meant to be played.

And I am thankful I had the chance to witness part of it, even the bitter end.

Tuesday night at the ball game, me and my dad had a helluva good time.

# Baseball's Spittin' Image

Watching baseball on television offers a rare opportunity to see the players up close. The Big Eye can put you nose-to-nose with your favorite stars, most of whom apparently do not shave on a regular basis.

Thurman Munson of the Yankees, for instance, looks like Pancho Villa after a two-week binge. Davy Lopes of the Dodgers looks like the guy who waters his horse.

The reason television has so much time to show close-up shots of the players during a game is there is a lot of standing around in baseball. Baseball is the only sport where three-fourths of the game is a time out.

Here comes the batter towards the plate. Watch him take a few practice swings, knock the dirt out of his spikes, fondle the tar rag, and scratch and adjust. (When a game is on national television, players should be reminded to cut down on the scratching and adjusting.)

There stands the pitcher on the mound. Watch him tug at his cap, pound the ball in the glove, pick up the resin bag, throw it down again, lean over for the sign, shake it off, nod agreement to the next one, and then throw over to first.

The batter steps out and here we go again, more practice swinging, dirt-knocking, and, if you must know, more scratching and adjusting.

Television even goes into the dugouts now. Dugouts used to be off-limits to civilians. A player could scratch and adjust and yawn and figure tax shelters until the last man was out, and who would know?

"Now," a ballplayer told me, "you have to act interested in the game for nine full innings."

Seeing the players up close on television during this year's Yankees-Dodgers World Series has also brought to my attention another interesting thing about men who play baseball for a living.

They spit more than anybody else. I don't suppose they spit on each other that much, but they spit on everything else. Home plate. The bases. The on-deck circle. Their hands. They used to spit on the ball, but that was outlawed. Leo Durocher once spit on an umpire.

Many baseball players chew tobacco. They all look like they have cheek tumors, but at least you expect them to spit. God help them if they didn't.

But watching the World Series games, I've noticed even baseball players who chew nothing at all also spit a lot.

Take Reggie Jackson of the Yankees. He spits constantly, even when he is figuring tax shelters in the dugout. He spits walking to the plate. He spits while he is there. He spits on balls. He spits on strikes.

Reggie Jackson spits with style. He has two distinct spits. There is the straight "ptui!" spit where he simply applies cheek and lip pressure.

His deluxe, superstar spit—typically flamboyant—is his through-the-teeth-line-drive-spit, however. He can fire away five to ten quick streams through the gap in his two front teeth faster than a Ron Guidry fastball.

One of the advantages to playing major-league baseball, I suppose, is it is one of the few professions that allows you to spit on national television and not be considered uncouth.

Other professional athletes don't have that luxury. Imagine Jack Nicklaus walking away from a putt on the scenic sixteenth green at Augusta and spitting. Basketball players wouldn't spit on a shiny hard-wood floor. Hockey players might spit on the ice if they had more teeth. Jockeys don't spit during horse races out of concern for their fellow riders to the rear.

A private citizen certainly can't spit in public. It is considered nasty, and it could spread disease. It's like a New Yorker mentioned to me recently.

"Strange thing about the subways in New York," he said. "You spit and they fine you twenty-five dollars, but you can throw up for nothing."

I really don't have anything against baseball players spitting. Maybe what bothers me is television insists upon showing them doing it close up.

Then, again, perhaps I should count my blessings. Television has gone face-to-face with the players and into their dugouts today. Tomorrow, the showers?

# Eighty Pound Lawsuit

I have always been a bit skeptical about organized athletics for children not old enough to have all their permanent teeth.

What is it about a society that will put a bat in the hand of a six-year-old, dress him in a baseball uniform, and ask him to perform on a diamond with real bases and everything, including umpires, coaches, and shouting spectators?

There is something called the "T-League." That's for kids who have just graduated from potty training. How can a child who hasn't learned his ABCs yet be expected to know to hit the cutoff man?

In the T-League, there is no pitcher. The ball is placed on a tee at the plate and the batter takes his cuts. Once I saw a T-League game where there was a close play at the plate. The runner was called out.

The runner's coach disputed the call. A grown man who would argue with an umpire at a baseball game involving toddlers is a sick person.

As the rhubarb continued, the opposing team's centerfielder became bored with the proceedings. He took off his glove, sat down in the outfield and began playing in the sand next to the fence.

Now, the other coach came storming out of his dugout. "Johnny!" he screamed to the youngster. "Do you want to play baseball, son?"

The child, still engrossed in the sand, studied his coach's inquiry for a moment, and then answered him by shaking his head, "No." Sand is marvelous when you are six, but it's lonely in centerfield.

I read an incredible story in the newspaper the other day about children playing organized athletics. It happened in Cobb County. Two midget football teams, nine-to-eleven year olds, play a game Saturday that ended in an 8–8 tie.

The winner would have gone on to the league playoffs that lead to an eventual "Super Bowl" championship. I am convinced adults organize children's athletic teams for their own enjoyment and glorification. Otherwise, who would care which team of nine-to-eleven year olds would emerge as champions over other teams of nine-to-eleven olds?

Since the game ended in a tie, neither team qualified for more play. Wait until next year, and let's all go home and play with the dog.

But, first, let's file a lawsuit.

Adults involved with the Mableton team claimed the other team, South Cobb, had hired its own officials for the game and had not gone by rules stating officials should be named by something called the Cobb County Midget Football Conference.

They wanted the game played over. They filed a protest to the conference. Protest denied. They hired an attorney. He asked a Superior Court judge to stop the playoffs until the matter could be settled.

"When you set up an organization, you say you are going to go by the rules," attorney for the plaintiff, Laurie Davis, told me. "But when there is a clear violation and nobody will listen to you, where do you go?

"Do you have a fistfight to settle it? No, you try to find somebody who will listen and make a fair decision."

That is Laurie Davis' explanation of why an issue involving eighty-pound football players was taken to court.

Good for Judge Luther Hames. Why he even agreed to hear the case is a puzzle, but at least he denied the request to stop the league playoffs and found there was no reason whatsoever for the court to get involved further.

Why not let children be children while they have the chance? Whatever happened to games where you chose sides and played in the yard and made up your own rules and never invited the overgrown kid across the street because he could hit the ball too far?

Whatever happened to damming creeks and climbing trees and playing in mud and marbles?

And what do you tell your ten-year-old son, the quarterback, when he asks, "Hey, dad, what's a lawsuit?"

## Boston

As I sit on my rump smoking cigarettes and typing this, I can still see runners coming in from the suburb of Hopkinton, twenty-six miles and 385 yards from the Boston Marathon finish line at the downtown Prudential Center.

It will be hours more before the last of the 7,800 official entrants, and maybe a couple of thousand more who ran anyway, finally come to the end of their exhausting journey.

The big names arrived to the cheering throngs what is now nearly two hours ago. Bill Rodgers was first. Actually, a cop on a motorcycle was first, but Bill Rodgers was right behind him with a record time of two hours, nine minutes, and twenty-seven seconds. It was his second straight Boston Marathon victory.

Appropriately, Bill Rodgers is from Boston and he sells sneakers. For accomplishing his feat, Bill Rodgers had a laurel wreath placed upon his head, and a medallion was hung around his neck by the governor of Massachusetts, Edward King. The crowd booed Edward King on Patriots Day in Boston.

What else the winner of the Boston Marathon gets is a bowl of beef stew. I hope they never change that. What occurred here Monday in cold and drizzling rain was a sporting event—a human event—that is still relatively pure and unspoiled by promoters and agents and television, not to mention candybar and beer companies that want to get their names in the newspapers.

Bill Rodgers crossing the finish line at the Boston Marathon Monday was as thrilling a moment as I have seen in sport. My goosepimples from the cold doubled in size.

But what is even more thrilling is watching now, watching the stragglers, the "nobodies"—the teachers, the housewives, the doctors, maybe even a cop or two, or Joe Futz the insurance salesman from Pottstown—push their tired and worn bodies to limits they probably never believed possible when they ended a two-pack-a-day habit and decided to become athletes.

Grown men are hugging each other at the finish line. Many are finishing in tears. A medical center is located in a nearby garage. Freezing, cramping runners are wrapped in cellophane sheets and placed on cots. Doctors move from cot to cot treating frightful blisters. It's the rescue center after an earthquake.

Asked a man who looked like he was dying, "Was it worth it?"

"I ran the sonuvabitch," he said, "and I beat it." On his soaked T-shirt were the words, "Human Power."

As I looked at him, I thought about Bob Horner of the Braves and Pete Rose and what's-his-name Parker with the Pirates and Reggie Jackson of the Yankees, as well as Jim Rice of the Red Sox, who at that moment was only a few blocks away at Fenway Park, lolling around in left field for something like fifty thousand dollars a game.

Columnist Leigh Montville of the *Boston Globe* was apparently thinking of the same sports millionaires' club when he so aptly advanced the Boston Marathon Monday morning.

"There are no agents involved today," he wrote. "There are no options being played out, no deals being made, no fleets of Mercedes being pulled into any special parking lot.

"The athlete of the day is an athlete, period, not some modern Clark Gable figure, some *Photoplay* sports god, cast in bubblegum and set atop some big rock-candy mountain.

"He is one of us again. As he runs the grand promenade from Hopkinton to the Prudential Center, he beckons us to come along, to sweat and enjoy....

"The runner in the eighty-third Boston Marathon returns fun and games to fun and games. Somehow, he makes the rest of the sports page seem silly on this day."

You sense the trend vividly here, the fitness trend that has 20 million Americans running, the trend that has the rest of us a t least thinking every time we light up a cigarette or spend another wasted, stinking afternoon watching overpaid balloonheads perform on that wretched talking box in our living rooms.

Grandmothers and grandfathers ran in the Boston Marathon Monday. A woman was telling her dinner companions in Boston Sunday night about announcing to her husband two years ago she was going to run in his race. His reply can't be printed here. But Monday, she showed him. There was a wheelchair brigade in the race. There were no fat people. A husband and wife, wearing matching outfits, finished together in an embrace.

Human Power. May the first promoter with the idea to turn this event into $100,000 Colgate Foot Race of Champions and move it to Las Vegas be shot at the next available sunrise, and may Howard Cosell never get close to it.

For the record, the Boston Marathon champion, Bill Rodgers, made a salary of seven thousand dollars last year selling shoes. He drives a dented, 1963 Volkswagen. He lives with his wife, and they pay $165 a month in apartment rent.

Somebody once asked him what he thought of golf as a sport.

"You get about the same exercise in a hand of canasta," he said.

In the same interview, he was asked if he thought Joe Namath was a great athlete because he could throw a football straight.

"I'll be running over his grave," was Bill Rodgers' answer.

# •On The Road

My favorite place to be is home. I know all the bartenders and where to get great barbecue. But a man can have an occasional high time in Memphis, the music is good in Dallas, Washington isn't such a bad place if you don't have to work there, and they like to hear me talk in New York. And once an angel cooked my breakfast in Tellico Plains, Tennessee....

# Cash Only

WASHINGTON • Here I sit in a big hotel room.

What fun.

When I was a kid, I liked hotel rooms because I could jump on the beds. Now, I like them because I can throw towels on the floor and somebody else will pick them up.

Washington is full of big hotels, because this is an important city and a lot of people from other places come here to work and to visit and to be politicians.

I suppose that the reason they always give you a booklet on security when you check into a Washington hotel is that there are lots of politicians here.

My booklet says, "Do not leave money, jewelry or other valuables in your room."

It also says, "Please bolt your door. This will shut out all keys. Also, insure that the security chain in engaged and that the connecting room door is locked."

Some rooms in Washington come with their own German shepherds. They are the ones nearest the Capitol.

This is a classy hotel I'm in. I knew it was classy when I saw the room service menu. The only thing cheaper than the $4.95 cheeseburger is a cup of coffee, which is $1.50.

One morning, I saw a fight between two taxicab drivers in the parking lot of my hotel. They were arguing about whose turn it was to pick up a fare. One driver bopped the other driver in the face, thus settling the argument. The other driver threw a rock at his colleague's cab as it sped away with the fare. Like I said, this is a classy hotel.

Hotel front desks are usually manned and womanned by young people who are very clean, wear expensive clothes and have a habit of acting snooty. Whatever happened to the friendly night clerk in his undershirt reading tomorrow's race entries?

Even the bellmen have come up in the world in today's hotels. The bellmen here wear red uniforms like the one Omar Sharif wore when he danced with Julie Christie at the Leningrad ball.

There is one staggering problem in hotels today, however. Hotels do not like to deal in cash. They abhor cash, as a matter of fact, along with anybody who would deface their front desk with it.

I deal in cash. Credit cards are financial heroin.

"May I see a credit card?" the snooty young woman at the front desk asked me when I arrived at my Washington hotel.

"Don't carry them," I said.

She called over the assistant manager.

"He doesn't carry credit cards," she said to him.

A lady behind me gasped in horror.

The assistant manager called over the manager.

"He doesn't carry credit cards," the manager was told.

I rattled my change as loudly as possible.

"If you don't have a credit card, sir," the manager asked me, his hands squarely on the hips of his designer trousers, "then how do you propose to pay your bill?"

Now, he had me.

"Cash," I said. "American," I quickly added, hoping to regain at least some face.

They wanted to see it.

A half hour passed before a decision was made. Finally, after I paid in advance, I was allowed to proceed to my room. They gave me a little card to read on the way up, however.

It said, "Because you have made a cash payment and did not present a major credit card at the time of your arrival, our operational procedure is to request that you make all further payments in restaurants, bars, and gift shop at the time the bills are presented."

The only time cash is accepted cheerfully in a hotel is when you give it to a bellman in the form of a tip.

After the experience of checking in, I followed a squatty version of Omar Sharif at the Leningrad ball up to my room.

He put up my bags, switched on the lights and the air-conditioner, and then waited impatiently by the door for his tip.

"Got change for a hundred?" I asked.

"No," he answered, "but I can get it from the front desk. I heard some yahoo just checked in using cash."

We both got a big laugh over that.

# Riding the High Lonesome

ON A GEORGIA RAILROAD • There are only two sounds out here. Four tires are humming as they hug the taxpayers' asphalt on Georgia 15. And the radio—God bless an automobile radio—has me in touch with you wouldn't believe the faraway places.

I am constantly turning the dial. Voices with no faces fade in and voices with no faces fade out. But at least there are voices, and without them the loneliness would creep even closer.

I have just departed from Sandersville, northbound through the deep-hole blackness the night brings to middle-eastern Georgia. There was a shooting in Louisville, clear-channel WHAS reports, but invading static keeps me from the details.

Dallas comes in loud and clear. It will be nice in Dallas tomorrow, with highs in the mid-seventies. I even pick up Cleveland.

You know they tried to recall the mayor in Cleveland. Now, the city council has been charged with accepting kickbacks. Things are tough all over.

Chicago's country WMAQ, an old friend, is beaming to thirty-eight states and Canada. A man sings a song that includes the line, "Plant them 'taters, and pull up another tomorrow."

It is difficult to avoid a hockey game, turning the dial on late-night radio. Hockey is enough of a problem for me in person. On the radio, it might as well be the noon news from Mars.

*"Ro-jay brings the puck to center ice! Marcham-bo checks him there. Jablare intercepts, and there is a whistle for icing the puck!"*

I am on the fringes of Hancock County, Georgia, listening to a man from Fort Wayne, Indiana, describe the actions of twelve foreigners on ice skates, chasing a rubber disc.

I turn back to Cleveland.

My headlights tunnel through the darkness. The tall pines frame the road, and two beady pearls of light suddenly appear in the distance.

This is the Halloween season, but a stray dog crossing the road has simply turned its head toward the lights of the car, and its eyes have reflected back.

Give me a dime for every stray dog on every Georgia back road, and my creditors can relax. I'll take a quarter for every dead possum.

I am trying to make Atlanta and home before sleep takes me over. Interstate 20 is somewhere ahead, just out of a place called Siloam in Greene County. The interstate is an auto jet-stream after crawling over two-lane. There is no other traffic because of the late hour and because country people have been in bed for hours. They get up early out here, you know. Don't let the sun catch you a-restin'.

There are tiny frame houses here and there, but not a sign of life to go with them. I grew up in a frame house that went dark at an early hour. The peace and comfort it held until morning has been difficult to relocate.

Downtown Sparta approaches. There are street lights, but no people. The old tavern in the middle of town, a historic landmark, looks haunted. It probably is.

Sparta lasts thirty seconds. The village of White Plains will be next. I cross Copeland Creek and Whitter Creek. There is a newscast coming in from WCAU, Philadelphia. Damn, I'm a long ways from Philadelphia.

What I am thinking is maybe everybody ought to do this occasionally. I am at least free with my thoughts here. Out like this, a man can talk to himself and it seems perfectly natural. You can ask yourself a question on a Georgia back road and get an honest answer.

Finally, Siloam. Siloam won't awaken for hours yet. The interstate approaches, laden with eighteen-wheeled monsters with big eyes and loaded backs bound for the city.

Parting with Georgia 15 is more difficult than I figured it would be. I will be home in just over an hour, but I realize that out on that primitive stretch I had maybe stumbled upon one of the modern urbanite's last escapes. I had ridden about all that remains of the High Lonesome on a pony with automatic transmission.

Cleveland has faded off the radio. I turn the dial again and a preacher is chasing the devil out of Tulsa. "Be saved or be damned!" is his warning.

Rolling along the interstate, I search for another hockey game.

# •Railroad Blues

One day there won't be any more trains to ride, and a part of me will die. The part that enjoys good conversation in the club car, morning coffee crossing the Potomac into Washington in the dining car, and little boys and old men who, as long as there are passenger trains, will stand beside the tracks and wave at them.

# Saying Good-bye

ABOARD THE SOUTHERN CRESCENT • I don't know exactly where we were. Between Spartanburg and Charlotte perhaps. Midnight approached. Four hours earlier, the Southern Crescent had pulled out of Atlanta's Peachtree Station bound for Washington with three green-and-gold engines, thirteen cars and a pack of riders come to attend the funeral-on-wheels of America's last privately owned overnight luxury passenger train.

"I just wanted to say good-bye in person," said a man who had boarded in Gainesville for the half hour ride to Toccoa.

There were three of them. The big one had a full beard, and he wore a cowboy hat. Somebody said his daddy was a big wheel with Southern Railway. You could have fooled me.

From somewhere in the back of the train they had each pulled out a guitar, and the music they were making had hushed what moments before had been a noisy, close-to-rowdy crowd that had gathered in the lounge car to drink its final respects to the Southern Crescent.

A black man and a black woman wearing white starched coats in the South tradition, poured.

Train songs. Naturally we wanted train songs. The guitar trio obliged. The big one with the hat and beard had a voice on him.

They began with "The Glendale Train." Somebody robbed it. They played "City of New Orleans," of course, and everybody sang along.

People took pictures. Channel 5 rolled its film. A girl got drunk and suggested we all greet the waiting passengers in Charlotte with a group "moon." The vote was close against her. A passenger ordered more beer for the singers, and I was in the middle of thanking the Lord for letting me be there when in walked Graham Claytor.

Graham Claytor is secretary of the Navy. Before Jimmy Carter gave him that job, he was president of Southern Railway and a fine friend to people who like to ride in passenger trains.

It was Graham Claytor who had insisted that the Southern Crescent continue running—and continue its excellence of service—when

27

all others around him wanted it stopped. He was a paying passenger this night, however. He had his own good-byes to say.

The big one cut down on "Wreck of Old '97," a damn fine train song, and Mr. Secretary of the Navy Claytor soloed to the top of his voice.

It was a poignant moment in the storied history of railroading.

He lingered with the passengers after his song. He even signed autographs, and he assured those who asked that Amtrak, which assumed control of the Southern Crescent Thursday, would continue the train's branch of service.

"This isn't the end of anything," Graham Claytor said.

But the Department of Transportation Secretary Brock Adams has proposed doing away with even the Amtrak version of the train.

"I don't think that will happen," said Claytor. "The political reality is this train will continue."

Another round for the singers, please.

Southern's plush office car number 11, fit for the company brass it carried, brought up the rear of the train Wednesday night. Atlantan Jack Martin, a power in the National Association of Railroad Passengers—the group that would like to hang Brock Adams—was on board. And somebody said they spotted Marvin Hamlisch. Marvin Hamlisch, among other things, wrote the music for *A Chorus Line.*

There were reporters and photographers and television people. And a group from Atlanta that would ride northbound to Salisbury, North Carolina, and then return on the final southbound Southern Crescent at 2:30 in the morning.

One Atlanta man had ridden the train from Atlanta to New Orleans Tuesday then boarded again Wednesday morning for the full trip back to Washington.

"It's my birthday present to myself," he said.

Southern also had extra security on the train. That was to keep souvenir-seeking passengers from stripping it. Extra security didn't help that much. Menus disappeared by the dozens from tables in the dining car.

So did napkins and coasters, and a sleeping-car porter was missing his platform stool.

"My God," said a conductor, "I'm glad the toilets are bolted down."

There was one ugly incident. A young woman who had driven from Jacksonville to Atlanta to ride the train had her purse stolen.

Security men finally located the culprit in a dark coach. They retrieved the purse and put the thief off the train in the cold and dark of Greensboro, North Carolina, at three in the morning, which is exactly what he deserved.

The Southern Crescent had been ten minutes late in arriving in Atlanta from New Orleans. With maybe a couple of hundred standing in the cold night to watch. The train finally poked its nose around the corner, gave a blast of its horn, and there was scattered applause.

"It's a sad day," said a man taking pictures.

Over the Peachtree Station loudspeaker came the Southern Crescent's final call. The caller sang it out: "Here comes the Southern Crescent, all the way from New Orleeeens!"

He added, "Thank you for riding Southern all these years." A touch of class.

All these years were 149 of them. Southern Railway opened regularly scheduled passenger service in the United States in 1830. The Southern Crescent was born the Washington and Southwestern Vestibuled Limited in January of 1893. Timetables advertised trips to Atlanta, the "Queen City of the New South."

Gainesville was the first stop Wednesday night. Then Toccoa, Clemson, Greenville, Partanburg, Gastonia, Charlotte, Salisbury, High Point, Greensboro, Danville, Lynchburg, Charlottesville, Culpeper, Alexandria and finally across the Potomac River into cold and windy Washington and Union Station. Twenty minutes later than the advertised 8:50 A.M.

There were no bands, no speeches. The train pulled in. The train stopped. The people got out. An era passed.

I own a book called *A Portrait of the Rails.* A man named David Morgan wrote the introduction. As I left the Southern Crescent for the last time Thursday morning, I thought about a line from that introduction.

The unmatched adventure of rail and steel is nearly over. I admit that. So does David Morgan. But at least he sounded hopeful when he wrote, "Oh, Lord, but it will take some doing for America to get that adventure out of her soul."

# • Ain't Love Grand?

Somewhere in this chapter is a column that expresses my feelings about homemade biscuits and their relationship to love and marriage. You would think a column like that would not make anybody mad. You would think wrong. They came at me with hatpins. One militant women's rights group wanted to chase me down Peachtree Street with large sticks. I have always considered myself an expert on women's liberation. In the last fifteen years, I have given two their freedom myself.

# Charlie and Julia

I called the Atlanta federal pen to inquire about Charlie Hines, Number 31579-120. Charlie, who is sixty-four, robbed a bank down in Florida a couple of years ago. After his conviction, he was shipped off to the "Big A."

"Yep," said a most unpleasant voice on the other end of the phone, "we still got 'im."

And probably will have for some time to come.

Charlie sent me something in the mail once. It was a copy of an article by a *Florida Times-Union* reporter named Ken Cruickshank. The article explained how Charlie became a bank robber.

I'll take the story from Cruikshank's article. He said he didn't mind.

Charlie got married in 1968 to a lady named Julia. Cruickshank told me, "They were a very devoted couple."

But hard times soon followed the marriage. Charlie had trouble with his feet. He was a diabetic. He had managed an amusement park in Tampa, but his health forced him to quit.

He bought some property in Tampa and opened a tavern and restaurant.

But Charlie Hines was in and out of the hospital and was eventually declared disabled by the Social Security Administration. He and his wife were trying to live on $156 a month.

In 1973 their problems worsened. Julia had to have an operation for cancer.

Charlie tried to go back to work to pay for her medicine. He tried a paper route of 125 miles for eleven months. Because of his health, he lost money on the route and was forced to quit again.

The bank took the tavern and restaurant away. Charlie turned sixty-two. His disability payments stopped. Social Security payments started. Now, Charlie and Julia Hines were trying to live on $137.10 a month.

Julia was in terrible pain, the story continues. Her medicine was expensive. Liquor was cheap. She began drinking heavily.

"I would mix her a drink to ease her," Charlie told Ken Cruickshank. "That's how it started."

Charlie's condition hadn't improved, either. He was having dizzy spells and periodic blackouts. A doctor ordered a brain scan.

"I couldn't do it, though," Charlie explained. "I didn't have that kind of money."

I was May 1977 and Charlie Hines was desperate. He borrowed a .22 pistol and took five times his normal amount of painkillers—"so I could walk"—and went out to look for a bank to rob.

He found one in Inverness, Florida. Charlie doesn't know exactly how much money he took. He never got a chance to count it. He was captured an hour later, fifteen miles away. He tried to plead insanity, but the jury wouldn't listen.

"I thought I was dying anyway," he said. "We had no food, no money and no prospect of getting any. So I went in and robbed that bank."

Last I heard, Charlie hadn't seen his wife since his interview with Ken Cruickshank. She can't come for visits.

Julia Hines, who accompanied her husband everywhere, was outside in the car that day while Charlie was inside robbing the bank.

Her number, incidentally, is 01129–179, Women's Unit, Lexington, Kentucky. She got fifteen months.

What made me think of Charlie and Julia was the exciting news that heiress Patty Hearst, who was also convicted of robbing a bank, had been freed from prison in time for her upcoming wedding to her former bodyguard.

It may be "the biggest wedding California has ever seen," said one news story, or just a "simple, private ceremony."

Whatever, they can afford it.

Let's all wish the happy couple well.

## Hope

ELLIJAY • The day has gown old gracefully in Ellijay, where the mountains are about to begin, and as is the custom in such settings, men with nothing better to do have gathered around the courthouse. In this case, it is the Gilmer County courthouse. There is a tree in front. And benches.

I still love a courthouse because it was on the steps of one I learned to play checkers and dominoes, and I learned about the Book of Revelation, which is what the old men would talk about after they tired of checkers and dominoes.

"Gon' be an awful day That Day," one old man would say at the courthouse.

"Gon' be a lot of folks caught short That Day," another would reply.

I even tried to read Revelation once. I stopped. It spooked me.

Standing with the men under the tree in front of the Gilmer County courthouse, I noticed the heat again—it remained stifling despite the approaching dusk—and perhaps that is what brought back Revelation's fiery warnings so vividly.

I am in Ellijay to watch the campaign tactics of Mary Beth Busbee, wife of the governor who is the first man in our state's modern history to seek a second consecutive term to that post.

I watch her closely and decide she loves her husband deeply or she wouldn't be working with such fervor. That feels good to me. He is campaigning south. She is campaigning north. Mary Beth Busbee says to people, "I'm Mary Beth Busbee, and I hope you will vote for my husband."

As I watch her, I think about marriage and how it has failed me— or how I have failed it—and I wonder if there is hope for those of us who have seen only marriage's bad side.

Earlier, Mary Beth Busbee had walked into a book and magazine store on the Ellijay courthouse square. "I'm Mary Beth Busbee," she said to the woman working there, "and I hope you will vote for my husband."

The woman spoke up quickly, "I lost my husband, you know. A year ago. He had a massive heart attack."

Mrs. Busbee listened. The woman's voice cracked with emotion. A year later, her voice still cracked with emotion.

The governor's wife introduced herself to the group standing at the courthouse.

A man in a T-shirt said, "If I was runnin' for office, the last person I'd want out tryin' to get me votes is my wife."

Mrs. Busbee wanted to know why.

"'Cause," the man went on, "She ain't never said nothin' good about me at home, and I know she ain't gonna say nothin' good about me out in public."

That brought a laugh all around. A good marriage needs a little levity, I was thinking.

Grady was there, and he met Mrs. Busbee, too. Grady is wearing overalls. His hat is twice my age. Remnants of the day's snuff encircle his mouth. For every courthouse, there is a Grady.

"Grady's ninety-three," somebody said.

"He still gets up and preaches over at the Holiness Church," somebody else said.

"That's my wife over there," Grady said to me. I looked and saw a little lady in a print dress, sitting on one of the benches alone. She drank water from a tall soft-drink bottle. There was evidence she dips now and then, too.

"How long you been married?" I asked Grady.

"Twelve years," he answered. "She's a good woman."

As I drove from Ellijay, I looked back once at the courthouse. Grady and his bride were walking away. It may have been my imagination, but I think I saw him take her hand.

Only one thing spooks me more than Revelation. Marriage. But Mary Beth loves George, a woman in a store grieves a year later, a husband makes a loving joke, and a ninety-three-year-old newlywed still feels the spark.

There is hope. There *is* hope.

# •A Stinking Place To Die

A good father. A good son. A good cop. A good friend. And a porno hustler who saw the light. Death and near-death from Guyana to Lawrenceville, Georgia.

# Mournful Silence for Steve Vann

On a cloudy day, spring's first rain approaching, they came by the hundreds to mourn the death of Steve Vann. One of the preachers got up and said, "This is the Christian act of mourning. That is why we are here."

The chapel was packed with people who had known him, who had loved him. Who still did. Perhaps now more than ever. The hallways outside the chapel were also crowded. Those who couldn't find standing room inside waited in silence outside. Grief is rarely loud.

He was seventeen. He was a senior at Lakeside High School in Dekalb County. He was a quarterback on the football team. He lived in an upper middle-class neighborhood. He had a lot of friends. He had parents who gave him their time and their attention and, of course, their love.

Saturday morning, somebody found him dead in a creek.

"There were all sorts of rumors going around," said a classmate at the funeral. "Somebody at first said he had been stabbed. I knew that wasn't true. If Steve had an enemy, I never heard about it."

The county coroner was on television trying to explain it. Steve Vann died of exposure to cold. He was found in creek water that had been below freezing the night before. The temperatures the night before were also below freezing.

Evidence of drugs were found in Steve Vann's body. There was no overdose, but there were drugs.

I talked to more classmates at the funeral.

"I don't guess anybody will really ever know what happened." said one. "He went to a party Friday night, but Steve just wasn't the type to take anything. He might have smoked some grass, most everybody else does; but I can't see him drinking and taking pills."

"Somebody could have slipped him something," added another. "I knew him as well as anybody in school, and he knew better."

The death has been ruled an accident. The most popular conjecture is Steve Vann, because of the drugs, became disoriented, wandered into the creek and remained there—unconscious—until the cold killed him.

Something like this shouldn't happen here, I was telling myself at the funeral. Look around you, I said. This isn't the ghetto. This is suburbia, good life America.

Steve Vann was no mindless punk.

He was an athlete. He was the second-string quarterback, but Lakeside is a state power with a huge student body from which to draw its talent.

"He had the best arm on the team," somebody said. "It hurt him that he wasn't a starter, but he threw a touchdown pass in one of the last games. He must have thrown the ball sixty yards."

But it happened. Steve Vann's death was drug-related. There is no way to hide it.

A young man standing outside the chapel said, between puffs on a cigarette, "If this don't make you think, nothing will."

I could make this a sermon. Parents tell your children. Teachers shout it. Drugs kill. What I had rather do is take you back to the funeral. There can be no more drastic lesson.

There were flowers, always there are flowers, and their scent inside a funeral home is a sickening sweet.

The casket was a metallic blue. There were flowers on top of it. The mother cried hard. The father appeared stunned. Old people hung their heads. Young people stared in disbelief.

An organ played softly. A man sang, "Will the Circle Be Unbroken?" and "I Come to the Garden Alone" and "The Lord's Prayer."

One preacher said, "We are all in shock."

Another said, "This is a great tragedy."

A third said, "He esteemed his elders, he respected his leaders, he was growing into a man of worth."

And at the end, the father walked to the podium and spoke from his breaking heart.

"If any of you are ever in trouble," he told his son's friends, "if any of you need any help, or need to talk, then come to me. This," he went on, looking at the casket before him, "is enough."

God bless him for saying that.

# Frank Schlatt: Don't Forget

The story didn't make the front page the other day, and I doubt the television stations even bothered with it. It was filled with a lot of legal-beagle mumbo-jumbo, and it didn't have anything to do with the price of oil, cracks in big airliners, or who's running—or not running—for the U.S. Senate.

"Slaton Appeals Ruling," whispered the uninspired headline.

So what? So this:

The story told about Fulton County District Attorney Lewis Slaton's efforts to convince the Georgia Supreme Court to reconsider a ruling it made May 31.

On May 31, the Georgia Supreme Court cited a technicality and overturned the murder conviction and life sentence of somebody named David Burney, Jr.

The court said that when David Burney, Jr. was tried, the trial judge had erroneously disallowed his request to act as his own co-counsel.

The legalese in the story was taxing, but from what I could gather, the trial judge had decided that since David Burney, Jr. already had two defense lawyers, granting him the right to act as his own cocounsel would have led to "undue disruption" of the trial.

District Attorney Slaton said a trial judge has the inherent authority to make decisions like that.

I don't know one end of a gavel from the other, and I would certainly hate to see David Burney, Jr.'s right to a fair trial violated, so I'm not about to take a stand for or against the Georgia Supreme Court's ruling.

After reading the story, however, I did want to bring up three other persons who have a fair stake in all this. They are the ones usually lost in the shuffle in such high-level maneuverers by men carrying law books. They come under the heading of "victims."

They shouldn't be forgotten.

There was Frank R. Schlatt, who was thirty-one. He was an Atlanta policeman. One day he answered a robbery call in a local furniture store.

David Burney, Jr. and three other goons were at the store. One of them blew off Officer Schlatt's head.

I went to his funeral. It was a pretty day and lots of people came. The chapel was packed. Fellow officers wearing white gloves stood at each side of Officer Schlatt's casket.

Somebody blew "Taps." Lester Maddox sat down front. High commissioners and police department czars arrived in limousines.

The preacher talked about what a good life Officer Schlatt had lived. I remember him trying to explain, then, how the Lord could allow such a good man to die. I forget his explanation.

At the graveside later, a policeman said to me, "We'll find the animals who did this, no matter how long it takes."

Then there was Officer Schlatt's widow. She was young and pretty. For a time, she held together well, but then the reality of the moment hit her again, and she cried hard and long.

God, there is nothing that tears at the heart like the sight of a young widow crying.

By her side under the funeral tent that day was Officer Schlatt's little girl.

What a brave little girl, everybody said. She was nine, I think. She fought off her own grief and tried to console her sobbing mother.

There was an American flag on Officer Schlatt's casket. Atop the flag lay a single flower. The little girl had placed it there for her daddy.

For as long as I live, I will never forget the moment an honor guard solemnly folded the flower into the flag and handed it to the grieving widow and daughter.

I don't really have an ending for his. I just wanted to make sure Officer Frank Schlatt and his family were at least mentioned while our judicial system contemplates how it can best serve David Burney, Jr.

# •Some Old People

Come to think of it, the one burning ambition in my life is to live long enough to become an old man...

## Smokey Bailey

The past few months had been good ones for Ottis "Smokey" Bailey, a friend of mine. Smokey Bailey is the man who collects Bibles and then gives them away to people he thinks "need a good talkin' from the Lord."

I first met him in the cool of a springtime evening as he sat in his favorite chair under some trees behind the big apartment buildings at 2450 Peachtree. Smokey worked there as the building custodian. He lived in the basement.

I come out here in the evenings," he told me, "to study the Book. Every answer to every question ever been is in the Book."

I wrote a couple of columns about Smokey, and you responded with hundreds of Bibles for him. He beamed each time I brought over a new load.

Later, I would see him on street corners from Buckhead to Brookwood, preaching to anybody who would listen—preaching to anybody.

There was the sweltering day in Buckhead. Smokey, long sleeves and a hat, stood in the park across from the old Capri Theatre, Bible held high in one hand, the other hand waving toward the heavens.

He was glad to see me.

"Done give every one of them Bibles away," he said. "Lot of folks out there got the Word wouldn't have had it if you hadn't brought me them Bibles."

I passed along the credit to those who had taken the time, who had gone to the expense to load Smokey's Biblical arsenal.

Smokey Bailey is nearly sixty. He's a color-blind black man without family, without a purpose other than to do what he thinks the Lord has insisted he do.

For his custodial work at the apartment buildings, he was paid two hundred dollars a month. Most of that went for new Bibles. He had layaway accounts at Buckhead book stores. Smokey was always busted, and Wednesday his world caved in.

There are several versions to the story. Aycock, the management company that runs Smokey's building, said Smokey was evicted Wednesday because the building owner, Mrs. Dorothy Johnson, instructed that it be done.

"He wasn't doing his job," said Garvin Aycock. "All I could do was what the law directs me to do."

Mrs. Johnson had no comment.

A resident who asked that her name not be used ("or I'd be evicted, too") said "A lot of it was racial. One of the men residents here complained that Smokey put his hand on some of the women's shoulders. He put his hand on my shoulder. And then he'd say, 'God bless you.'

"There wasn't that much work for Smokey to do in the first place. Mrs. Johnson didn't like him preaching either. Whatever else Smokey was, he was harmless. What happened today broke my heart."

Smokey was fired from his job and kicked out on the street. A half-dozen sheriff's deputies came and moved his meager belongings from his basement apartment out to the sidewalk on Peachtree.

Smokey *had* been warned. His checks had been stopped. "I didn't know where else to go," Smokey told me later. "I didn't know they would do me that way. That ain't no way to do anybody."

People from Atlanta's Housing Support Service came to help Smokey. They hired a truck to move away his belongings. Bibles were scattered up and down the sidewalk. A chair wouldn't fit in the truck. A passerby stopped and purchased it for seven dollars. The movers gave the money to Smokey.

He was eventually taken to the Salvation Army, which has agreed to house him for ten days. Somebody paid to have his few possessions stored.

I can't place any blame here. Maybe Smokey should have spent more time on his custodial duties before heading for his streetside pulpit. And he did have notice that the eviction was coming.

But an old man with a big heart and a message of love is homeless today, and that makes me sick to my stomach.

I do remember something Smokey said to me once, however. It had to do with not being overly concerned with personal gains and security while running in the human race.

"Money ain't never worried me," he said, "'cause my wages are comin' later. The Lord's been holdin' 'em for me."

# Pauline Jones

Pauline Jones had enough troubles as it was. She is crippled and in a wheel-chair. Arthritis. She was married once, but that was a long time ago. There were no children.

She has two sisters in Atlanta, but they have health problems of their own. They can't help. Pauline in sixty-eight. And she is alone in the city.

What keeps her going is her stubbornness. You need that, and a good measure of it, when you fight The Big Red Tape Machine.

Two months ago, she entered a hospital for surgery on her legs. Doctors say there is a possibility she may even walk again. Pauline is still in the hospital going through a period of rehabilitation.

But it has been slow. Slower than normal because she doesn't know if she will have a place to live when the hospital releases her.

It all began months ago when the Atlanta Housing Authority ordered her to leave her apartment at the AHA high-rise at 2240 Peachtree.

The other tenants were complaining. Mrs. Jones drinks too much, they said. She gets frightened in the middle of the night and calls the fire department, they said. And she keeps cats in her apartment. There is a rule against pets in AHA apartments.

Pauline wouldn't budge. "Somebody poisoned one of my cats," she says. "I had two kittens left in my apartment. They are all I have."

The AHA took her to court. Tenants from her apartment came by bus to testify. The jury ruled she must leave. Her attorney managed to hold off any further action by appealing to a higher court. Recently, the higher court ruled against Pauline Jones again.

She got that bad news in the hospital the other day from her own law firm, which decided to inform her in a rather matter-of-fact letter that also mentioned she might be evicted within ten days. Pauline didn't need that. "Physically, she is coming along fine," said a doctor at her bedside. "But psychologically, all this hasn't helped a bit."

I talked with two lawyers and one housing authority spokesperson about Pauline Jones this week. "We had no choice," they said. "We had the other tenants to think about. We even offered her another apartment, but she wouldn't take it." Graciously, the AHA says it will not evict Pauline from her apartment until the higher court sends down its final order to the lower court. "Then," said the spokesperson, "we will proceed."

The AHA's suggestion for Pauline Jones is a private nursing home.

I looked to finger a heavy here, but I don't know exactly who it is.

The housing authority is legally within its rights to evict resident Pauline Jones. The other tenants, just as needy, were howling. Fire trucks in the middle of the night aren't exactly what elderly people living in a high-rise apartment building need to see.

And the AHA had offered Pauline another place to live. It had warned her of the consequences if she didn't vacate.

And she *is* stubborn, and she *is* eccentric, but at sixty-eight, she has every right to be.

She doesn't understand how bureaucracies work, and she doesn't understand legalese. And the thought of moving frightened her.

And when it gets lonely in the night, who can begrudge her a drink and a couple of cats to keep her company?

And when she asked me last week, "Where will I go when I leave the hospital? How can I afford a nursing home on $188.40 a month?" I didn't have an answer for her.

It's a big-city dilemma. An urban-living standoff. Nobody to blame. Nobody to go to for help. And a little old lady nobody seems to want is caught squarely in the middle of it all.

**B**y 1980, Lewis Grizzard had become a bit of a sensation. TIME magazine called him one of the "rising newspaper humorists in the country," and Kathy Sue Loudermilk was still selling its way off the shelves. So, Grizzard's second book, Won't You Come Home, Billy Bob Bailey?: An Assortment of Home-Cooked Journalism for People Who Wonder Why Clean Underwear Doesn't Grow on Trees was greeted with a great deal of anticipation. And the fans weren't disappointed; Grizzard continues in the tradition of Kathy Sue Loudermilk, offering up another compilation of newspaper articles that touch on a variety of issues, from church fans to the dangers of living alone. Two themes also appear in Billy Bob Bailey that will become very familiar to Grizzard fans in the later books: his fear of doctors ("The Doctor, Revisited") and his love of dogs ("Buddy").

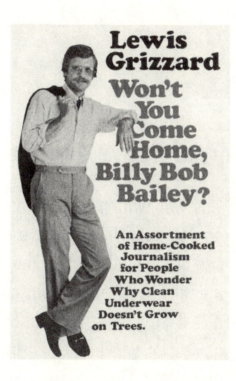

**Lewis Grizzard**

**Won't You Come Home, Billy Bob Bailey?**

An Assortment of Home-Cooked Journalism for People Who Wonder Why Clean Underwear Doesn't Grow on Trees.

1980

# •Take My Advice...Please!

This was written before I got married—again—which will all be explained at the end of the book. But for those of you who are still living alone, or who are planning to give it a try, there would be some excellent advice for you here. Like the part about underwear. Clean underwear doesn't grow on trees, you know.

# On Living Alone

I'm not certain who digs up such information, or who pays for the digging, but there was an item on the evening news about more and more Americans living alone these days.

I can think of at least three reasons for that:

1. People are waiting around longer before they get married.
2. Those who didn't wait around to get married are getting divorced in droves.
3. Maybe there are more nerdy-type people who can't find any-body who will live with them.

I am sort of an expert on all this because I live alone. I could go into details as the why, but that isn't really necessary. Just check somewhere between aforementioned reasons-for-living-alone "2" and "3."

A lot of people actually enjoy living alone. There are certain advantages:

1. People who live alone can leave their underwear lying around all over the floor.
2. There are never any arguments over what to watch on television. If you live alone, you can even watch "The Dating Game," and who will know?
3. The phone is always for you.
4. You never have to hear, "Honey, there's something I've been meaning to talk to you about," when Dallas is fourth-and-one on the Washington two-yard line.
5. If you find a hair in your soup, you know for certain whose it is.

I could go on, but those are the highlights. Perhaps what I am trying to say is, if you are sharing a dwelling and think you would like to kick the bum or old bag out, think twice.

The item on the evening news went on to say people who live alone tend to die younger than others.

I think I know why. I can only speak for the male of the species, but there are certain shocks that will come the minute she's gone, fellows.

49

Let's go back to the underwear for a second. You probably think your underwear walks to the washing machine, dives in, and after washing itself, marches back to your dresser, gets inside, and folds itself.

Soon after I was cast adrift, I wore all my underwear once, and then looked in the dresser for another fresh pair. My underwear was where I had left it—lying around all over the floor.

A man of my standing and upbringing certainly wasn't going to wash his own underwear, so I did a second-time-around on the dirties. After that I had no choice. I went to K-Mart where they were having a special and bought a six-month supply of undershorts.

When they were dirty, I did what any other just-divorced American male would do. I threw them away and bought another six-month supply.

There are other similar problems. Toilet paper and fresh towels don't grow in the bathroom. Strange green things do if you don't clean it, however.

Light bulbs. Light bulbs will drive you crazy. They are always burning out. You have to take the time from your busy schedule to go out and BUY more light bulbs and then bring them home and screw them in. That alone can take years off your life.

Food. You live alone, you try cooking for yourself. You cook for yourself, you can get poisoned, and then there are the dishes. You don't cook, you eat a lot of heat-and-serve Mexican dinners, which annually kill thousands of men who live alone.

Beer cans. Who is going to throw his own beer cans in the garbage? Let me tell you something about beer cans. You leave a couple of empty beer cans around, and the next time you look there will be four beer cans, and then eight, and pretty soon, you are up to your eyeballs in empty beer cans.

If you are about to strike out alone, big boy, I don't mean to frighten you with this, so to soften the blow, maybe I should offer one more advantage to living by yourself:

If you do happen to die young, maybe the end will come before you finally have to break down and change your sheets.

# •Great Issues

**Sports Cars: Pro and Mostly Con:** If you are currently thinking of buying a sports car, read this. Afterwards, if you still want to buy a sports car, you deserve one.

**People Who Talk to God:** I received a great many nasty letters after writing [this]. Anytime you mention God, I have discovered, you get a lot of nasty letters.

**Me and My Guccis**: Sometime later, someone stole the very pair of Guccis I am writing about here. I left them in the locker room of where I play tennis, and when I returned, they were gone, which made me feel very good. At least one person I hang around with at the tennis courts has some class. I never would have guessed it.

# Sports Cars: Pro and Mostly Con

Sooner or later, everybody goes through the stage of wanting to own a sports car. I think it has something to do with being deprived as a child.

I had plenty to eat as a child, and I was warm at night. But I never had the real necessities, like a trip to Europe after high school graduation or a sports car.

I have owned all sorts of cars. My first car was a red-and-white 1956 Chevrolet. Tennis racquets cost more today than I paid for my first car.

I have also owned a Volkswagen, several Pontiacs and a Vega. Of all the cars I have owned, the Vega is the one I have never forgiven.

It was brown and hard to crank. I used to park it in bad neighborhoods and leave the keys on the hood, hoping somebody would steal it.

Somebody tried once. I was hiding in a nearby alley watching with a pair of jumper cables just in case. When the Vega wouldn't crank, I appeared with the jumper cables and offered my services to the thief.

"Forget it," he said. I gave him taxi fare home for his efforts and called a tow truck.

I finally got rid of my Vega by giving it to my ex-wife. I am a bad person.

A year-and-a-half ago, I decided it was time I had my first sports car. The eagle inside me cried for the opportunity to soar.

Get the picture:

*The open road lies ahead, begging to be conquered. I wind my way along it, two steady, gloved hands sure upon the wheel of my classic new sports car. The sleek lines are unmistakable. The perfectly balanced hum of the engine is a purr.*

*I pass through Barletta as a streaking blur. And on through Trani, Bisceglie Molfetta, toward Monopoli, along the Italian shore, the blue waters of the Adriatic shimmering in the sun.*

*My road hat sits deftly upon my head, tilted at precisely the correct, cocksure angle. My scarf treads the breeze behind me. As the road straightens, I press the toe of my right Gucci against the*

*accelerator, and the naked eye cannot still the motion I command.*
   *The woman beside me? A long and most unbelievable*
*story, my friend. It began only a fortnight ago as I stood on*
*the balcony of my hotel room in Roma....*

Picture that in a brown Vega that won't crank and has a lot of empty beer cans in the hatchback.

The sports car I finally bought is a British import, one of those sexy little numbers with the racing stripes and plaid seat covers. The man who sold it to me is from Tupelo, Mississippi, and chews gum. His leisure suit matched the seat covers of the car.

"Sassy chassis, ain't it?" he remarked as we looked at the car. Somehow, I thought buying a sports car would be like shopping for rare art treasures. It ain't.

I am now an expert on sports cars because I have owned one for a year and a half.

Here are the advantages of owning sports cars:
1. They're cute.

Here are the disadvantages of owning sports cars:
1. Sitting in a shoebox is more comfortable.
2. Try finding somebody to work on one a hot Sunday afternoon in Cooper, Texas.
3. While riding with the top down it is impossible to talk, smoke, listen to the radio, or keep the part in your hair. Also, bugs occasionally fly into your mouth at sixty miles per hour.
4. A lot of silly teenage girls have one, too.
5. If you hit a trailer truck head-on in a sports car, they'd be lucky to find all your movable parts in a week, despite a three-county search.

What I am trying to say here is I have passed through my sports car stage, and it was a miserable experience. The latest bad thing to happen was Tuesday morning. I was backing out of my driveway, and the steering wheel broke off the column.

Luckily, the car came to a halt against a large tree. I don't know where the steering wheel finally landed.

And in order to leave this with a clear conscience, I must also admit I never drove along the Italian coast or the shimmering Adriatic.

I made all that up on the way to work today. My neighbor's cleaning woman gave me a ride in her Vega.

## People Who Talk to God

I have just completed reading a newspaper interview with a woman named Margaret Schroeder of Murphy, North Carolina, who has written a book about the fact she talks to God.

Everybody who believes in prayer can make that claim, of course, but Mrs. Schroeder says God talks back to her. As a matter of fact, she says that in the past ten years, God has sent her thirteen thousand personal messages.

Her book is entitled *Love, Acts of the Apostles*, and it costs $3.95, a rare bargain. If I were getting personal messages from God, I would write a book, too, but I would charge a sight more than $3.95 to let the rest of the world in on our conversations.

Mrs. Schroeder says her messages from God have to do with such things as the importance of loving one another, sacrifice, and eternal life.

I am not going to say I think Mrs. Schroeder is trying to pull a fast one, because I don't doubt much of anything these days. Billy Carter stopped drinking, the mayor of Chicago is a womanperson, and a baseball team from a foreign country has challenged for a spot in the World Series.

But I must admit I have always been a bit skeptical of people who say they get messages from God.

There was a man in my hometown who claimed to have gotten a message from God—Uncle Jake Gaines, the laziest man in town. One Sunday morning, Uncle Jake stood up in church and described his experience.

"His words were written across the sky," he began. "They said, 'Uncle Jake—go preach the gospel.'"

You never know, so they let Uncle Jake preach the morning sermon. Billy Graham he wasn't.

After the service, my grandfather took Uncle Jake aside. "I think you may have misread the message, Jake," he whispered. "You sure god didn't say, 'Go plow your corn?'"

What else bothers me about people who say they talk to God, like Mrs. Schroeder, is they never get any specific information.

One of the messages Mrs. Schroeder says God sent was, "Body is a great sounding board; it is the mystic chord struck by the mind."

If God decided to give out information to twentieth century mortals, I frankly don't think He would beat around the bush.

I honestly do not want this to come off as overt irreverence, but after reading about Mrs. Schroeder, I couldn't help making myself a list of specific questions I would like to ask, given the opportunity for two-way conversation with the Almighty:

What REALLY happened at Chappaquiddick? It's urgent.

How long before you do something about Howard Cosell?

Is disco a sin?

Is there life after gasoline?

Has Anita Bryant become a total embarrassment?

Did Elvis go to heaven?

Can rabbits swim?

Is Oral Roberts on the level?

Does the name "Margaret Schroeder" ring a bell?

# Me and My Guccis

All my adult life, I have attempted to rise above my humble beginnings. Take shoes, for example. Now that I have steady work and live in the city, I like to wear nice shoes.

In the boondocks, we didn't wear shoes unless it was an absolute necessity. Like your feet would freeze if you didn't, or there was a funeral.

My boyhood friend and idol, Weyman C. Wannamaker, Jr., a great American, didn't wear shoes even on those occasions, but he did wash his feet twice a week whether they needed it or not.

The first time I saw Weyman in a pair of shoes they were forced upon him.

We were in the sixth grade, and the teacher organized a field trip to Atlanta to hear a performance by the symphony orchestra. As the bus pulled away from the school, she noticed Weyman was barefooted.

Horrified, she ordered the bus driver to stop at the nearest shoe store, where she bought Weyman a pair of shoes. He protested, but the teacher hit him in the mouth and Weyman didn't mention the shoes again.

During the performance of the symphony orchestra, however, Weyman's feet began hurting him, so he took off his shoes and hung his bare feet over the railing of the balcony. Unfortunately, he was between washes.

The entire percussion section and two flute players stopped in the middle of Chopin's Movement No. 5 to search for what had obviously passed away days earlier.

I always think of Weyman when I pull on a new pair of shoes. Lately, some of the fellows down at the lodge have been giving me the business because I now own a pair of stylish loafers by Gucci, the famous Italian leatherperson.

I prefer to think their boorish, catty remarks stem from ignorance, sprinkled with at least a tad of jealousy.

"I knew him," said one of the buzzbrains, wearing a pair of hideous lace-ups named for something you eat with fried catfish, "when he wore high-top tennis shoes and ran rabbits."

How utterly crude. And untrue. I wore low-cuts.

My new Guccis were a gift from a lady friend who brought them back from Palm Beach, where they have a Gucci store. They don't have Gucci stores except in spiffy places like Palm Beach. It's easier to move an NFL expansion franchise team into town.

My lady friend is always bringing me nice gifts when she goes on trips. Once she went to the drugstore and brought me a giant bottle of mouthwash and some extra-strength Tegrin shampoo.

I must do something nice for her. Maybe I'll take her bowling.

What makes a pair of stylish Italian loafers by Gucci so appealing is their softness, their master workmanship, and their price.

I've bought cars for less. Walk into a Gucci store, and they ask for your shoe size second. First, they want a quick glance at your Dun and Bradstreet.

Not just anybody can wear a pair of Gucci shoes, of course. Those crass dolts down at the lodge, for instance.

"You get a purse, too?" cracked one of the sorry lot, a hint of white socklet peering outside the top of his brogans.

Disgusting.

My new Guccis are an unpretentious oxblood, accented perfectly with buckles and slightly raised heels.

The cushioned inner soles wear the proud Gucci crest with the subtle, but effective announcement, "Made in Italy," as if there were any doubt.

When I am in the company of individuals with the proper breeding to appreciate such hallmarks of style, I am not hesitant to remove one of my new shoes to prove I am wearing the Real McCoy.

"Have you noticed I am wearing Guccis?" I asked the hostess at a dinner party.

"Frankly, I haven't," she said.

I took off one of my shoes and showed her the proud Gucci crest on the cushioned inner soles. I didn't want to stay at her stupid dinner party anyway.

I also called Weyman C. Wannamaker, Jr., back home and told him I am now wearing Guccis. I knew he would be proud.

"You wearing them shoes," he said, "is like putting perfume on a hog."

## Shafting the Kids: Part II

There was no such thing as sex education when I was in school. I take that back. There was plenty of sex education in my school, but classes were conducted behind the grandstand of the baseball diamond and the teacher usually had only a couple of years on his students.

We did have "health" classes in school. That is where you learned clean fingernails are important, if you don't brush your teeth regularly your teeth will fall out, and you can get all the Vitamin D you need by spending a lot of time out in the sun.

We also had biology classes where we did hear something about sex, but only if it involved a couple of frogs.

But times changed. Educators finally began to realize that perhaps the reason so many of their female students were getting pregnant—

some at ridiculous ages like twelve and thirteen—was because all they knew about sex was the basics of how to perform it.

So, gradually, sex education has been introduced into many of our schools. There has been protest, of course, because some parents and school board members still think it best for children to learn about sex in other places.

Like behind the grandstand of a baseball diamond.

Take Cobb County, for instance. They are always fighting about something in the Atlanta suburb of Cobb County. This time, it is whether to introduce a unified sex education program into the sixth, seventh, and eighth grades.

Those in favor of the program argued at a recent school board meeting that it is important because an estimated thirty thousand American girls under the age of fifteen will get pregnant this year.

Those against the program had a good argument too. Cobb County school board member John McClure said students need less sex education and more teaching of "self-respect, discipline, and patriotism."

He also suggested sex education be handled in the home.

"But not everybody has a home," countered a Cobb County high school senior who came to the meeting.

"Hmmmp!" said board member McClure, who could be suffering from chalk dust on the brain.

We think nothing of teaching our children all about wars. Half of the time I was in school, I was learning about a war, the third Punic all the way to the Great WWII.

People get maimed and killed in wars. Sex has to do with loving. Teach 'em about war, but ignore the little brats when they ask about sex.

The new sex education plan didn't pass at the Cobb school board meeting. The vote was 3–3, but the superintendent has already said he would not ask his teachers to teach the program if the board were split on such a "controversial issue."

I don't know if this will help, but it is probably worth a try. For those Cobb students who will be deprived of sex education for at least another year, here is my own sex short-course.

Clip and save:

• Having sex, even if you are only twelve, can make babies.

• Having a baby while you are still a kid is a bummer.

- If you are determined to have sex no matter what anybody tells you, there are ways to avoid making a baby. They are called "contraceptives." Ask an older friend who won't go berserk how to obtain them.
- There is nothing dirty about sex. It is a beautiful and necessary part of life.
- Many grown people would be better off if they realized that.

# • It's Been One Hassle After Another

**Looking For Mister Goodwrench:** How many days does it take me to screw in a light bulb? Four. Three to fool around with it myself, and one to round up an electrician to finish the job.

**The Doctor, Revisited**: My doctor read this and called me in for an immediate reexamination. I was sore for a month.

# Looking for Mister Goodwrench

A man from the city water department came to my house last week and cut off my water. He had some absurd reason for doing that. I think he mentioned I hadn't paid my bill on time.

I attempted to explain. Maybe there were some goats in the neighborhood, and one was nosing around in my mailbox and ate my payment to the city water department.

You can't explain *anything* to a man with a wrench.

So there I was for a couple of days, with no water. It was a learning experience.

I learned it is virtually impossible to brush your teeth using orange juice.

I learned if you wet your face with milk and then try to shave, the pain will be incredible.

I learned if you don't shower for a couple of days, you won't have to put up with worrisome people like your friends and fellow employees.

I learned if you don't wash coffee cups, something green will grow inside of them.

I also learned that I still don't know anything about anything that is mechanical in nature. I couldn't change the oil in my salad.

Here's what happened:

I finally reached the city water department—the telephone there had been busy for forty-eight hours—and the woman who answered agreed with me that it was probably all a big mistake that my water had been cut off.

She apologized on behalf of the mayor and the city for the inconvenience and said if I would pay my bill, along with an additional six-dollar service charge, the man with the wrench would return to my house and turn the water back on.

Naturally, I accepted her apology and her kind offer to right the department's wrong.

I returned home that evening, expecting to find running water.

Instead, I found a note in my door from Mr. Goodwrench.

"Dear Sir," it began, "I turned the water back on in your meter. However, I left it off in your property valve because of an indication there was a faucet open in your house.

"You can turn the water on in your property valve. It is located approximately twelve inches down in a metal pipe that is located approximately ten feet behind your water meter. Thanks."

Thank you. But I don't know anything about water meters and property valves. I can barely operate my shower curtain.

I called the water department again, and they tried to explain to me where to locate my property valve. They tried to explain it several times.

"You'd better talk to Mr. Something-or-Other," a woman said. Mr. Something-or-Other became impatient and said, "If you don't know where your property valve is, you'll just have to look in your yard until you find it."

It was raining outside. I searched for my property valve for half an hour. It occurred to me that I wouldn't know my property valve if it walked up to me and played the flute.

I called the department again. It was after five o'clock Friday afternoon. I went into Plan "B." I started crying.

Another half-hour search, and I finally located what I determined to be my water meter. It was located in some tall grass I should cut, but when I pull the starter cord on my lawn mower, nothing happens.

I walked approximately ten feet behind my water meter and, sure enough, there was a metal pipe like the note said. I reached twelve inches inside it and, sure enough, there was my property valve, along with a lot of dirt and bugs and worms.

I suffered a mild coronary, ruined a shirt and a pair of pants, but I finally found my property valve and immediately felt a sensation of great satisfaction.

I went back inside my house, took a shower, and watered the green things growing in the coffee cups.

# The Doctor, Revisited

It had been a long time since my last complete physical examination, and I was in no hurry to have another one.

When I was eleven, a doctor examined me from head to toe before my trip to Camp Thunder and pronounced me fit for everything from overnight hiking trips to towel fights in the shower.

I didn't want to go to Camp Thunder and secretly hoped he would find some horrible malady like bumps on my head, which would have kept me away from camp and couldn't have been as bad as the towel fights in the showers there.

A towel fight in a shower involves inflicting physical harm upon a fellow camper. My boyhood friend and idol, Weyman C. Wannamaker, Jr., a great American, was the king of the towel fighters.

He would wet one end of a large beach towel and fling that lethal end toward the uncovered hindparts of his victim, snapping it back on impact with a resounding, "whap!"

Bend over to retrieve your soap in a shower with Weyman C. Wannamaker, Jr., and his beach towel, and you would be standing for campfire vespers the entire week.

I had no bumps on my head when I was eleven, and I went on to Camp Thunder. I solved the towel fight problem. I didn't take a shower for seven days.

I sat alone at campfire vespers. But I sat.

I don't know what came over me last week to have another physical examination. Doctors spook me. Their offices spook me. Their nurses spook me, and all their receptionists just got off the boat from Transylvania where their last jobs were in a blood bank.

"You vil take a seat, please," they begin. "It vil only be a little while."

It vil never be a little while. It vil be an eternity if you are as frightened of doctors as I am. Doctors' offices even smell like impending doom.

Last week, while I waited for my doctor, I tried to read a magazine. Why are magazines in doctors' offices always out of date?

I picked up a *Newsweek*. Roosevelt was on the cover. Teddy.

My doctor was a nice enough fellow. First, he asked me a lot of questions.

Do you smoke?

Yes.

Do you drink?

Yes.

Do you eat regular, balanced meals?

No.

Do you get plenty of rest and exercise?

No.

Do you ever get dizzy spells?

Only when I run out of cigarettes or have a drink before "The Today Show" goes off the air.

Then, he took me into a small room with only one door, which he closed, and examined me. He examined my head, my nose, my ears, my throat, my neck, my chest, my back, my stomach, my legs, my feet, and my toes.

I still don't have any bumps on my head, but one of my toes has an ingrown nail which he mashed, prompting a scream. That is how he pays his receptionist. She loves screaming.

He did other things to my person as well, but I can't mention any of them here except to say they were indignities that shouldn't happen to a rabid dog.

"It's for your own good," the doctor said.

Jack the Ripper told his patients the same thing.

Later, he turned me over to a nurse who put needles in me and gave me an X-ray. I have also wondered why, if there is nothing dangerous about X-rays, the nurse who administers them always stands behind a lead screen?

The doctor didn't put it in so many words, but I suppose I will live.

Otherwise, the receptionist—Countess Rubellina in the old country—wouldn't have asked, "Vil you be paying now, or shall ve bill you later?"

"Later, sweetheart," I said. "Later."

# •Stray Dogs and Sweet Memories

**"Buddy"**: I get sentimental about dogs. I can't help it. If you have ever looked deep into a dog's eyes and felt he was urgently trying to give you a message, then maybe you will understand what I was feeling when I wrote the following.

**Ode to a Church Fan**: After this column appeared in the newspaper, I received nearly a hundred church fans in the mail. This sort of work does have its benefits.

# "Buddy"

ON A BACK ROAD • My grandfather would have called the dog a "sooner."

"Just as soon stay in the house as out," he would have laughed.

The day was ending, but a long drive home remained. I had stopped for gasoline in one of those all-purpose country service stations, the kind where there is always a little boy with a dirty face and a dog hanging around.

The little boy was buying milk for his mother. The dog was yawning and scratching.

"That your dog?" I asked the old man pumping the gasoline.

"Took up here," he said.

"Fine-looking dog," I went on.

"Smart, too," said the man. "Watch this."

He locked the pump to "on" and walked over to the dog. He held out his hand, and the dog responded by lifting a paw. Smart as a whip, that dog.

"How long you had him?" I said.

"'Bout a week," said the man.

"Any bother?"

"Not a bit. I figure somebody put him out of a car. That little boy that was here buying the milk wants him, but his mamma won't let him bring the dog home. Says every dog he brings home gets run over, and it upsets the little boy something awful."

That was an instant memory. I had a losing streak with dogs, too.

There was "Snowball." Every child eventually gets a furry white dog named "Snowball." My daddy bought me mine the day after he got back from Korea. "Snowball" got it from a laundry truck.

"Butch" was later. He chased cars. One day, he caught one.

The vet said "Pokey" had pneumonia. He allowed me to pet my dog one last time, and then he took "Pokey" into a back room, and I never saw my dog again.

I had "Plato." Now there was a dog. I lost him in a divorce settlement, believe it or not. I gave up dogs after that. Missing a dog is a worrisome pain.

"This dog got a name?" I said to the man at the station.

"I call him 'Buddy.'"

The old man scratched the dog, and "Buddy" nuzzled close to the source of affection.

I petted the dog myself. He was obviously of a generous mix, a young dog with patches of white and yellow and black. I tried the paw trick, and "Buddy" responded on cue. Impressive.

I like dogs because they forgive easily, know little or nothing about revenge, and will settle for thirty seconds of care and attention if that is all you have to spare.

I have a house and it is empty, and I have considered adding a dog to the premises. But then I decided that is foolish because I often sleep where I fall, and I do not want a lonely dog on my conscience.

I paid the man for the gasoline and started to get back in my car. The dog was staring at me, or maybe it was just my imagination. Regardless, I stared back.

"You like that dog, don't you?" said the man, smiling.

"That's a fine dog," I said.

"Why don't you take him with you? I got another dog at home."

I gave him five or six excellent reasons why I couldn't and drove away.

It's been a week now. It was dark that night and I wasn't familiar with the road. I doubt I could ever find that country service station again, even if I wanted to.

Which, you understand, I don't.


# Ode to a Church Fan

Somebody took a poll the other day concerning how Americans feel about going to church during these trying times, and the published results said the takers and the leavers were split something like fifty–fifty.

I polled myself and decided I still enjoy going to church because it's OK to sing out on the choruses, but there are some things about the modern church that bother me.

In some churches, for instance, sermons are shortened during the football season so nobody will miss a one o'clock kickoff, and let us all stand and sing the first and third verses of "Drop Kick Me, Jesus, Through the Goalposts of Life," which, in case there are any doubters, is a real song.

You can also tithe with a credit card nowadays, and that seems almost too convenient and impersonal, and most churches—even the little white frame country churches where you can still hear an occasional "Amen!" from the back row—have adopted progressive attitudes toward air-conditioning.

So it's more comfortable in church today, but air-conditioning giveth, and air-conditioning taketh away. Gone for good are those paper fans with the wooden handles that were always available in the hymnal racks on the backs of pews.

It never bothered me to be hot in church because I thought being hot in church was a part of God's Great Plan. Sweat it out, brother, because that's just a sample of what awaits the backslider.

Down home on an August Sunday morning, the church is packed, and the congregation squirms as one.

You can *feel* the fire. You can *smell* the brimstone, and the closer the preacher gets to the everlasting flames, the faster the fat ladies in their print dresses fan themselves.

But there were other uses for church fans besides fanning away the Devil and the dog-day heat. You could swat noisy children and flies with church fans.

"Goat" Rainwater used to chew on the wooden handles, but "Goat" was always chewing on something like pencils or crayons. My mother said he probably had a vitamin deficiency.

A person could also learn a lot from a church fan. I learned what heaven looks like. The fans in our church were provided by the local funeral parlor, and at election time, a politician or two would bring in a batch.

On one side of a church fan would always be a picture of Jesus sitting with children and a lamb or two and a pony in a soft meadow near a brook.

That was obviously heaven to an eight-year-old, and I would stare at that picture during the sermon and wonder if pony rides were free when you crossed over Jordan. Certainly, I finally decided. That's why they call it "heaven."

On the other side would be the commercial message of the funeral parlor or the politician who had placed the fans.

"Hillside Funeral Home. All Insurance Policies Honored. Twenty-four Hour Ambulance Service. Ask About Our Chapel Rates."

Or, "Elect Buster Knowles State Senator. Veteran. Family man. Deacon. Honest."

Buster Knowles wasted a lot of money providing church fans, because he was never elected. He always included his smiling countenance on his fans, and he looked too much like the crooked Indian agent on "Tales of Wells Fargo."

Fortunately, I have what is probably one of the last church fans. A person who knows of my concern for their demise gave me one, and I am forever in his debt.

One Sunday soon, I may even take my fan to church, and in case the sermon runs a little long, I can stare peacefully at the picture of heaven while the rest of the congregation sweats through a hell of a thought:

God and Jimmy the Greek forbid, but if the preacher doesn't stop in five minutes, there goes the opening segment of "The NFL Today."

**D**on't Sit Under the Grits Tree with Anyone Else But Me *arrived in 1981, with the Reagan years well underway. Everywhere Lewis Grizzard looks, things seem to changing—like the Springlake Pharmacy, home of real limeade and the drinkable milkshake, which succumbs to "progress" and simply ceases to be. Other things are as annoying as ever, like banks, with their oppressive quiet and constant lack of usable pens. Grizzard focuses squarely on the present and doesn't flinch, but his remembrances of his youth and the things he has loved and lost bring a touch of bittersweet poignancy, a combination that is now firmly established as his trademark writing style. Grizzard dedicated* Don't Sit Under the Grits Tree *to his publisher, saying "To Helen Elliott who believes in angels."*

1981

# •Social Studies

If you hang out around salad bars, work in a bank, have a cute name like "Traci," speak a foreign language, are a professional athlete who says, "Hi, Mom" when you're on television, are overweight, slurp your soup, jog, are a lardbutt, wear padded bras, or don't like old-fashioned soda fountains, maybe you'd better pass up Chapter One and go directly to Chapter Two....

# All Quiet in the Bank

I often have wondered why more people don't suffer nervous breakdowns when they go into banks. Each time I go into a bank, I emerge with sweaty palms and a pounding heartbeat.

That is because each time I go into a bank, I become so frustrated that I want to rant and rave and scream, but it always is so *quiet* in a bank, which is something else that frustrates me.

Why should people be quiet in a bank? I can understand being quiet in a library or in a funeral home, or even in a doctor's office because there are sick people around, but what's the big deal about keeping your voice down in a stupid bank?

What could they do to you if you suddenly started making a lot of noise while standing in line waiting for a teller?

Is an officer of the bank going to come out from behind one of those wooden doors with the brass nameplates and say, "I'm sorry, sir, but you will have to deposit your money in another financial institution if you can't learn to be quiet while you are in our bank?"

Of course not. Banks just have conned us into thinking they are some kind of big deal where you have to whisper and wear deodorant like when you're in a fancy-smancy restaurant.

Standing in line in a bank is just like standing in line at the grocery store waiting to buy tomatoes. You can chat and sing and even make sucking noises through your teeth and they're still going to sell you those tomatoes because they want their greedy hands on your money.

Next time you're in a bank, break into "The Star Spangled Banner" and I promise nobody will do a thing, except that maybe a few people in your line will think you're nuts and leave the bank, and then you will be able to get to the teller more quickly.

That's something else that drives me crazy about banks. When they build banks, they always build a lot of teller windows. I bank at a small bank. There are maybe ten teller windows at my bank.

Never in the history of my bank have there been more than five tellers behind windows at one time, and three of them always have

"Next Window Please" signs keeping customers away while the line stretches out the front door.

If there are ten teller windows, why can't there be ten tellers? Where ARE the other tellers? Probably back in the vault being beaten for making an effort to hurry through transactions with less than fifty people waiting in the line.

But let me tell you what REALLY cracks me up about banks. Their pens. The ones that are chained to the penholders that are nailed to the desks where you are supposed to fill out your deposit slips.

Every time I go into my bank, it's the same with those pens. I go to the first desk and one of the penholders is empty because somebody has ripped off the pen.

So I pick up a second pen, but it doesn't work. I shake it, rub it across the paper a couple of times, and shake it again. Still, it doesn't work.

I go to the second desk. Same problem. Either the pens have been lifted or they don't work.

Why, I have complained, can't a bank maintain a couple of pens that work? And how can I trust a bank to keep my money safe when it can't even keep an eye on a couple of crummy pens?

But nothing ever changes. The next time I go into my bank, the pen situation will be the same, there still will be two tellers for ten windows, the line will be long and you would think somebody just had died the way everybody is being so careful to whisper.

If I had the guts, I would start making sucking noises through my teeth and fill out my deposit slip with a pink crayon.

## Running With Rosie

I admit I never had much interest in running until recently when I found out you can cheat at it. Now that I know you can cheat, I accept running as being a real sport.

Heretofore I thought it was just something bored housewives and guys who were in the drama club in high school did occasionally because they had never known the joy of sweating.

You can put in the fix in practically all our favorite athletic competitions. Baseball had its Black Sox scandal, basketball its point-shaving of the fifties, and somebody is always stealing a playbook in football, or doping a horse, or shooting an East German swimmer full of strange hormones.

But running? I never thought anybody cheated at running. I remember when some of my friends first started running.

"Who pays tennis or softball?" said one, an out-of-work actor. "Running is *pure,* man."

But then we come to the case of female runner Rosie Ruiz, the first woman to come across the finish line at the Boston Marathon, the Super Bowl of running.

Other runners, including the woman who finished second to her, and spectators claimed Rosie had not run the entire 26.2-mile course, but had slipped into the pack two miles from the finish line for a record time and a victory that is reportedly worth a lot of bucks in endorsements. Pure, man.

The stink caused a number of subsequent investigations and news conferences and a great deal of confusion. The problem, of course, is that the sport of running never has had to deal with a cheating scandal before and wasn't equipped to handle it.

What running needs to circumvent any such embarrassments in the future is a set of guidelines to follow in checking out finishing runners to make certain they completed the entire course.

The National Union for Running Development has offered a standby list of methods to be considered.

Following are some of the NURD suggestions:

- FOOT TEST: After twenty-six miles, a runner's feet would emit a certain odor. Each finishing runner will be asked to allow a foot judge to smell his or her feet. If the judge is rendered unconscious, there is a good chance the runner completed the entire course.

- JOGBRA TEST: No qualified female runner would attempt twenty-six miles without an official "jogbra." All the top women runners wear them. Any female finisher without such equipment should be detained for more questioning. Any male runner wearing a "jogbra" should be detained, period.

- SHOE TEST: Runners finishing in sandals, disco boots, moccasins, anything a cowboy might wear while walking the pasture, or barefooted would be considered suspicious. Any runner finishing in flip-flops should be placed in the same holding cage with the guys wearing "jogbras."

- BREATH TEST: Finishers who reek of Gatorade or orange juice probably are legitimate. Finishers who reek of gin or vodka probably are just drunks who wandered out of the nearby bar to see what all the commotion was about.
- BURMA SHAVE TEST: "Burma Shave" signs will be posted every five miles along the course, and each finisher must be able to recite what appeared on each sign in order. For instance:

  *Here Sits Rosie,*
  *Brokenhearted.*
  *She Finished Fine,*
  *But She Never Started.*
  *Burma Shave.*

# One Limeade for the Road

The Last Soda Fountain. Put it up there with *The Last Picture Show,* a marvelous motion picture, and with "The Last Cowboy Song," currently a raging country hit where Willie Nelson joins in on the last chorus.

But The Last Soda Fountain in neither a movie nor a song. It is reality.

The place was Springlake Pharmacy, and it was located near my home in Atlanta. There are memories.

Springlake Pharmacy is where I met Barney, my all-time favorite wino. Barney would sit outside Springlake on a slab of concrete and pour out his bottled dreams from a brown paper sack.

There was the day I saw two punks, they were maybe ten and eleven, throwing rocks at Barney. Barney wasn't bothering anybody. Barney was just drifting away for a time, and he was too weak and too drunk to dodge the rocks.

I chased the kids away. Barney thanked me by asking for a dollar.

Barney is dead now.

Springlake is where I bought toothpaste and shampoo and cough syrup and newspapers and once, when I forgot a rather special Valentine, one of those gaudy red boxes of chocolates she pretended to appreciate.

Springlake was where a person could belly-up to the counter of an honest-to-god, just-like-back-home-in-a-small-town soda fountain and ask and receive delights the likes of which are rare and precious indeed in the urban eighties.

Milkshakes. Not milkshakes out of some machine you have to eat with a spoon. That's not a milkshake. At Springlake, you got a milkshake constructed by a human hand scooping real ice cream into a cup with real milk, and you could *drink* the darn thing, as the Lord intended.

Limeade. Real limeade, made out of real lime juice, hand-squeezed from real limes. Thousands of limes were rendered juiceless over the years in Springlake. As far as I know, there is no other place in the continental United States that serves as good a limeade as did the soda fountain at Springlake.

I could go on. Cherry Cokes. Coca-Cola syrup, carbonated water and a shot of cherry juice. Good hot dogs. Ham sandwiches with thinly sliced tomatoes.

And nobody behind the counter wore stupid uniforms, and they didn't sell cookies in a funky little box, and the chicken noodle soup was called "chicken noodle soup." At some fast-food establishments today, chicken noodle soup would be called "Soup McNoodle."

My old pal, Estin, was numero uno behind the Springlake soda fountain counter. He spoke only when a grunt wouldn't do just as well. And then there was the lady who worked with him. I never got her name. Somebody said she was Estin's niece. One day I ordered a ham sandwich and some potato chips from her. She delivered the ham sandwich. She forgot the potato chips, which were located on a rack behind the counter.

"You forgot my potato chips," I said.

"You got two legs," she replied. "Get your own potato chips."

It was that sort of friendly service that kept me coming back to Springlake, hallowed be its name.

Springlake, thirty-odd years at the same location, closed recently to the sound of a bulldozer's snort. A new shopping center went up next door, and the Springlake building was sold, and the Springlake owner decided to move his pharmacy and to pass the soda fountain along to the ages.

I walked inside for one last look.

"We're all just about in tears," said a lady helping dismantle the shelves. "It's a sad day."

The Last Soda Fountain. Let us mourn its leave, for nothing similar remains to take its place.

"Soup McNoodle." How utterly disgusting.

# •Cordie Mae and The Gang

It has been my pleasure to have known a lot of great, and near-great people in my time: Cordie Mae Poovey, Hog Phillpot, Kathy Sue Loudermilk, Mavis Boatright, all the Rainwaters——especially "Spot" and "Goat"——the late Curtis "Fruit Jar" Hainey, and my boyhood friend and idol, Weyman C. Wannamaker, Jr., a great American, who first showed me my way around a 1957 Chevrolet....

# Making Sense of the Census

What I like most about the taking of the census is that it's fair. Once every ten years everybody counts, and everybody counts the same:
One.

Even Bo Derek. Imagine, Bo Derek a "one." Somehow, I can't imagine that.

Something else I like about the census: It's thorough. Most Americans probably mailed in their census reports April 1, but canvassers soon will be going into places like pool halls, dives, and fleabag hotels in big cities to count heads.

That is important because, otherwise, a pool shark or a wino could be missed. The last time there was a census, for instance, my boyhood friend and idol, Weyman C. Wannamaker, Jr., a great American and part-time pool shark and wino, wasn't counted. He was taking a nap (passed out) underneath a load of turnips in the back of his pickup truck when the census-taker came around.

I can't wait for the results of the census to be released. I realize a great deal of the information we gave the government is supposed to be kept confidential, but this census thing is costing the taxpayers a bundle, so why shouldn't we be privy to some of the juicier material?

I just happen to have with me a list of questions I would like answered by the census:

- The 1980 census had the audacity to ask people if they have indoor plumbing. Did any of my neighbors mark "no?" (I have always suspected the Bloomingraths. They spend an awful lot of time going back and forth to Mr. Bloomingrath's "tool shed," and they never have any beer parties.)
- Does anybody really live in North Dakota?
- What is the population of my hometown, Moreland, Georgia? The last time there was a census taken, there were 300-plus, but that was before the Rainwater family moved out. (There were so many Rainwaters, they ran out of names for the last four children and had to name them after dogs in the neighbor-

hood. "Spot" Rainwater was one of my closest friends.)

- How many teenagers are there in America, and when will they all grow up so rock music will finally die out?
- Ten million people live in New York City, where the air is foul, the streets are dirty and the weather is terrible. Hardly any body lives in Yellville, Arkansas, where the mountain air is refreshing, there are many streams and rivers for fishing and boating and swimming naked, and you don't have to lock your doors at night. Why?
- Who is the oldest person in America, and has he or she ever jogged?
- Under "sex," how many people put down "undecided," and are any of them in my tennis club?
- How many people in America are named "Engelbert Humperdink"?
- Did the name "D.B. Cooper" show up anywhere?
- When is my wife's birthday?
- And, finally, just exactly how many people do live in this country, and with the government doing the counting, how can I be certain that figure is correct?

I can't. If the government knew beans about simple arithmetic, it wouldn't just now be balancing its own checkbook for the first time since it was taking the 1960 census.

Incidentally, they missed Weyman C. Wannamaker, Jr., in 1960, too. He hid in the family "tool shed," which used to be none of the government's damn business.


## "When It's Refill Time in Heaven"

I stopped for lunch in one of those meat-and-three vegetables places the other day and, much to my surprise, the waitress brought my iced tea in a quart fruit jar.

You don't see that sort of thing any more, but fruit jars have a significant history, and I even get a little sentimental when I think about them. More about that later.

First, for those who are not familiar with the fruit jar, it is a wide-mouthed, glass container normally associated with the process of canning, as in the canning of vegetables and fruits.

These containers also may be called "Mason" jars for the name of the company that produces state-of-the-art fruit jars. But people who say "Mason jar" instead of "fruit jar" probably are a little snooty and sleep in pajamas.

In the past, in certain parts of rural America, it was quite common for people who couldn't afford regular glassware—and slept in their underwear—to use these fruit jars as part of their table setting.

You take a family in my hometown, the Rainwaters. The Rainwaters were too poor to afford glasses, so Mrs. Rainwater always served beverages in fruit jars.

Claude "Goat" Rainwater was one of my best friends, despite the fact that he rarely bathed. Mrs. Rainwater would serve Goat his food and his fruit jar on the back porch with the dog.

There are certain advantages to drinking from a fruit jar.

The wide mouth allows easy intake of the liquid inside the jar, whether it be iced tea, buttermilk, lemonade, or something more potent.

It is so easy to drink from a fruit jar, as a matter of fact, that it is virtually impossible to keep whatever you are drinking from pouring over your chin, down your neck, and onto the front of your shirt.

There was a man who lived in the woods near my hometown who sold a certain beverage that was so potent you wanted to be careful not to get any on your shirt because it would ruin your shirt. It would eat through sandpaper and cut out engine knock, too.

As I finished my lunch and poured down the last of my iced tea from my fruit jar, my sentimentality got the best of me as I thought of one of my favorite people from my youth.

I am speaking of the late, great Curtis "Fruit Jar" Hainey. Fruit Jar got that name because he was never without one stuck in his coat or in his back pocket.

It usually was filled with the clear liquid-and an occasional bug or leaf the strainer missed-that he purchased from the aforementioned man in the woods.

I can see ol' Fruit Jar now, ambling along.

"Where you headed, Fruit Jar?" we would ask.

"Refill time," he would answer, smiling and holding up his empty jar as he headed for the woods.

Fruit Jar spent so much time drinking there was a notch on his nose from where the top of his jar pressed against it.

"That stuff's gonna kill him someday," the women from the church used to say.

Sure enough, it did. He went one jar over the line one cold night. The blind girl wrote a song for him and sang it at the funeral after the preacher got through. She called it "Lord, Remember Fruit Jar When It's Refill Time in Heaven."

Goat Rainwater even took a bath for the services. A man like Curtis "Fruit Jar" Hainey doesn't die every day.

# •Boy Columnist

There are many lessons to be learned from the following chapter, such as how to inspect the cap of a wine bottle before you screw it off, where to get a good tattoo, what to do with your polyester leisure suits, how to tell whether or not something that goes bump in the night is about to get you, and where grits come from. This is a very intellectual chapter....

# The Secrets of My Past

My admiration for Dan Rather, heir to CBS anchorman Walter Cronkite, went up a notch when I read he had admitted in an interview with *The Ladies Home Journal* he has used heroin.

"Not socially," says Rather, but "so I could write a story about it" when he worked in Houston.

Rather also said the experience was "a special kind of hell."

It is only right that a newsman of Rather's stature, who is entrusted with the faith and admiration of millions who watch him dole out the evening news, makes public any previously hidden incidents in his past that could be unveiled later and possibly cause him to lose credibility and respect.

We ask our politicians to open their backgrounds and checkbooks to public scrutiny, so why shouldn't we expect the same from our newspersons?

I'm glad I asked that question, because I am here today to make my life an open book, just like Dan Rather.

As a reader, you have every right to know whether I am a sane, normal person or whether I am some kind of dope-headed sicko who probably has been arrested a couple of times and doesn't like football.

We will do this in the form of an interview. First question, please:

**Q.** Have you ever "experimented" with drugs?

**A.** Yes. As part of a general science project in the seventh grade, I fed my neighbor's cat six bottles of aspirin to see what effect the six bottles of aspirin would have on a cat.

**Q.** And your findings?

**A.** After eating six bottles of aspirin, a cat will lie very still.

**Q.** You are evading the real question here. Have you, yourself, ever indulged in an illegal drug, such as marijuana?

**A.** I cannot tell a lie. Once at a party in Chicago I was with some weird people, and the host, who wore a lot of neck chains and didn't button the front of his shirt, passed around a marijuana cigarette to all his guests.

When it came my turn, the cigarette was very short. I attempted to smoke it, but I sucked the fire into my mouth, instead.

Marijuana causes large blisters on your tongue, so I don't smoke it any more.

**Q.** Have you ever been arrested?

**A.** No, but once I received a substantial penalty for early withdrawal from my passbook savings account. The bank teller hit me in the mouth.

**Q.** Have you ever undergone treatment for a psychiatric disorder?

**A.** That was in the third grade when the county health teacher was called in to question me concerning why I wouldn't go out of the building during recess to play with the rest of the children.

**Q.** And what did the health teacher find was your problem?

**A.** I was scared stiff of Cordie Mae Poovey, the meanest girl in school, who used to pound on my head during recess because she didn't like my looks.

**Q.** Do you ever drink to excess?

**A.** Only on weeknights. On weekends, I get blitzed.

**Q.** Are there any abnormal sexual tendencies in your background?

**A.** No, but I had a cousin who was a thespian.

**Q.** Is there anything more you would like to add to this investigation?

**A.** Just one more thing. When I wrote this column I was high on a plate of Uncle Sam's Red-Hot Texas Chili.

# Dr. Feelbad

I was browsing through the papers when I ran across an interesting, but alarming, statistic: twenty percent of the medical costs in the country are being paid out by hypochondriacs—people who are convinced they are sick, but nobody will listen to them, especially doctors.

I have been a practicing hypochondriac for years, and I can't begin to tell you of the suffering. I have had symptoms of every known disease, but never have I been able to find a doctor who agrees with my diagnosis.

Like the time I had toe cancer. Toe cancer is when your little toe becomes swollen and sort of bent out of shape and hurts when you walk.

I went to my doctor, convinced my toe would have to be removed that afternoon, but hoping the leg, at least, could be saved.

My doctor took one look at my toe and said my shoes were too tight. So I changed to a half-size larger shoe, and my toe got better, proving loose shoes to be a definite cure for toe cancer.

This twenty percent thing bothers me because that is a bundle of money for hypochondriacs to be paying out to doctors to be told nothing is wrong with us. Hypochondriacs don't go to doctors to be told nothing is wrong: they go to be assured something most certainly is.

I think I have a solution to the problem. Rather than a doctor, what hypochondriacs need is another hypochondriac—like me, for instance—to tell them they are just as sick as they think they are, which would make them very happy. And think of the money they would save in doctor bills.

Maybe I could write the first newspaper advice column for hypochondriacs. They send in their symptoms, and I use my many years' experience diagnosing my own health problems to diagnose theirs.

Let's give it a practice run. I'll be "Dr. Feelbad, the hypochondriac's best friend," and the column would work something like this:

**Dear Dr. Feelbad**: After playing tennis, I get a terrible pain in my elbow. My doctor says all I have is common "tennis elbow." But I think it is something much worse. Which of us is correct?
                                    **—D.A., Pittsburgh, Pennsylvania**

**Dear D.A.**: You are. What does your doctor know about tennis? You don't have tennis "elbow." You have tennis "arm," and it probably will have to be amputated eventually, and you won't be able to play tennis. You will become a recluse and have to sit around staring out the window all the time. Have a nice day.

**Dear Dr. Feelbad:** I have a terrible headache. My wife says it is because I got smashed last night, but I know better. I know it probably is a brain tumor and I won't live until morning. How do I break the news to my wife?
                                    **—Checking Out, Mobile, Alabama**

**Dear Checking Out**: Your diagnosis is absolutely correct. But wait until you and your wife are in bed and then break the bad news to her gently. But don't keep her up too late. Remember, she has to get up in the morning. You don't.

**Dear Dr. Feelbad**: I know the seven danger signals of cancer, and I worry about them all the time. But are there any others I could be worrying about, too? I'm getting bored with the first seven.

—**Betty, Laredo, Texas**

**Dear Betty**: You bet your boots there are. Here are some of my other favorite danger signals to worry about: Drowsiness toward midnight, increase in bellybutton lint, and sudden loss of memory after a half-dozen tequila shooters.

**Dear Dr. Feelbad**: Last evening I experienced chest pains and difficulty breathing. Incidentally, my girlfriend, Bearnice, who weighs three hundred pounds, was sitting on me at the time. Could I have heart trouble?

—**Slim, Terre Haute, Indiana**

**Dear Slim**: Probably not. Bearnice's last boyfriend wrote in about the same thing, but all his problem turned out to be was four broken ribs, bruised kidneys, and a squashed liver. Sorry, better luck next time.

## Cooter Brown Award

The time has come to announce the winner of the First Annual Drunk-As-Cooter Brown Award. The award is named for the immortal Cooter Brown, who could get drunker than anybody.

Once Cooter got so drunk he wandered into the middle of a church service and began babbling incoherently.

"Praise the Lord!" somebody screamed out. "That man is speaking in tongues!"

"No, he's not," said somebody else. "It's just Cooter Brown trying to sing, 'There Stands the Glass.'"

"There Stands the Glass," I might explain, is a Webb Pierce classic, a favorite of many a drinking man.

This award, conceived by me, neither encourages nor condones drinking, but I do feel if someone distinguishes himself in that area, he should not go unrecognized.

The winner of the First Annual Drunk-As-Cooter Brown Award goes to a fellow I know, Rigsby, who got so drunk on a recent business trip that he checked into his hotel twice.

"Nobody gets that drunk," I said.

"Yes, they do," said Rigsby, "I got off the airplane, went straight to my hotel and checked in. But I didn't go to my room. I met some business associates in the bar, and we proceeded to drink for several hours.

"We got pretty much oiled and decided to go somewhere for dinner. I drove my rental car. I parked it in front of this brick wall.

"When we came out of the restaurant, after dinner and some more drinks, I cranked the car, the accelerator stuck, and I went smashing into the brick wall."

"Anybody hurt?" I asked.

"No," Rigsby replied, "but the car was totaled."

"What did you do then?"

"Well, my associates suggested I push the car away from the wall, call the police, and tell them that while I was in the restaurant, my car was smashed and whoever did it drove away."

"Did the scheme work?" I inquired.

"I think the police were really going for my story," said Rigsby, "until they found the brick in the grillwork of the car."

"Did they book you?" I went on.

"For being drunk, of course," Rigsby explained, "and also for carrying a concealed weapon."

"A concealed weapon?"

"You're not going to believe this: I had ordered a steak for dinner, but I couldn't eat it all. So I asked for a doggie bag. I also thought of the fact that if I was going to eat the rest of my steak later in my room, I would need a knife.

"When nobody was looking, I slipped a knife into my inside coat pocket. I tried to explain that to the officers, but they didn't believe me, especially since I had been so intent on taking the knife, I had forgotten the doggie bag with the rest of my steak in it."

His associates, Rigsby said, finally were able to obtain his release in the wee hours of the morning. He took a taxi back to his hotel.

"I was still drunk," he said, "so I checked in again. It was the next morning before I discovered I had two keys and two rooms. I should never have drunk those six tequila shooters."

The selection committee (me) already is looking for candidates for next year's award. If you think you or somebody you know qualifies, enter soon. Remember, the bigger the fool you made of yourself, the better chance you have to win.

"I'll drink to that," said Rigsby, whose latest escapade was getting soused and losing his rental car.

"I parked it somewhere in the Midwest," he explained. "I just can't remember which state."

Cooter Brown, rest his soul, would have been proud.

# True Grits

I was hoping that four years of Georgian Jimmy Carter in the White House would finally clear up the matter of grits. Grits have been so terribly misunderstood by people who are from parts of the country other than the South.

But, alas, Georgia's Jimmy is only a few weeks from departing Washington in favor of Californian Ronald Reagan, who wouldn't know grits from granola, and I fear grits will never cross the gap that has left so many yet unaware of the history and many uses of one of America's most interesting foods.

As one of the nation's leading experts on grits (my mother served them every morning for breakfast), all I can do is try to light the way for those still blinded by prejudice and fear.

Grits won't bite you. Grits taste good and they're good for you. Just sit back and relax and put yourself in my hands and let's go. "DISCOVERING GRITS: GRIZZARD'S GUIDE TO A SOUTHERN DELICACY FOR FOLKS FROM NEW JERSEY AND PLACES LIKE THAT":

- The origin of grits:
Cherokee Indians, native to the Southern region of the United States, first discovered grits trees growing wild during the thirteenth century. Chief Big Bear's squaw, Jemima Big Bear, is said to have been out of oatmeal one day, so she gathered the tiny grits growing from the grits trees and cooked them in water for Chief Big Bear.

    After eating the grits, Chief Big Bear ordered his squaw, Jemima, burned at the stake.

    Later, however, Southern planter Jim Dandy found grits taste a lot better if you put salt and pepper and butter on them. Grits really took off in the South after that. Today, grits orchards may be seen from the Carolinas to Florida and west to Louisiana.

    At some orchards, tourists may "pick their own grits." If you decide to give it a try, make certain each grit you pick is ripe and firm. Raw grits tend to stick to the roof of your mouth and have been known to choke even large goats.

- How grits got their name:
From the Cherokee word, *greyett*, which means "corn pebbles." The Cherokee thought grits were tiny versions of corn. They even tried to make bread from grits, which brought about another big run on squaw-burning.

- What does the word "hominy" mean?
It is Southern for "Blended voices," as in, "That quartet sure has nice hominy, don't it?"

- How to prepare grits:
First, go out to your grits trees and pick a peck of grits. Wash, then allow to soak in warm buttermilk for an hour. Add two tablespoons Jack Daniel (Black Label) Tennessee sippin' whiskey and one cup branch water.

    Stir, bake at 450 degrees for approximately one hour. Cover with sawmill gravy, add butter, then salt and pepper to taste. Cheese (Kraft American) optional.

    Must be served hot. Cold grits tend to get gummy. You wouldn't serve cold, gummy grits to communist sympathizers from New York.

- What are some other uses for grits?
Patching blowouts. Snake bite. Bathroom caulking. In some parts

of the South it is even believed grits will grow hair. This is doubtful. Grits do make a delightful party punch, however. Just add more Jack Daniel.

- How can I order my grits tree?
  By sending $38.95 for each tree desired to "Grits-a-Grow-Grow," in care of me. Add $15 if you want to take advantage of our special offer for our handy "Grit-Picker," which will save time and wear and tear on your hands when you go out to gather your grits off your new grits tree.
- What else may I order from "Grits-a-Grow-Grow"?
  A special brochure outlining how you can purchase valuable vacation property at our new Alligator Point resort in Florida and about six zillion copies of Amy Carter's Washington Coloring Book. Order now while they last.

# •Ordinary People

The best stories are true stories, the real stories about real people....

**Townsend:** Jim Townsend died soon after I wrote... [this] piece. I'm convinced he is presently in Heaven, trying to con Hemingway and Voltaire into doing something for the new magazine he's starting.

# Good News

Earl Sheriff, sixty-eight, is custodian at the little high school in the village of Fredericktown, Ohio, which is near Columbus.

You ought to hear them talk about "Mr. Sheriff" around the school.

"He's the sweetest, kindest, most helpful man I've ever known," one of the teachers was saying. "We couldn't get along without him."

Still, nobody knew much about Earl Sheriff's background until one day when some of the students, who were in the midst of a course called U.S. Wars, casually asked the custodian if he knew anything about WWII, the Big One.

Earl Sheriff knew quite a bit. He had lived through it, as a matter of fact, and the students asked him to come and lecture the class.

So here is the school custodian lecturing in the classroom, and Sgt. Earl Sheriff talked about how he had served as a light machine gun section leader and how he had hit Utah Beach with the 121st Infantry as part of the first replacement unit in after D-Day.

He also mentioned fighting through the hedgerow country of France and into the Hurtgen Forest. And he brought along his Purple Heart—he was wounded three times—and his Silver Star and his Medal of Luxembourg.

"The light machine guns went ahead of the infantry," Earl Sheriff told the students. "We were up there where we could look the Germans in the eyes. It was hell, but we had a job to do, and we did it—and a lot of good boys got killed."

An old soldier remembers, and today's high school students, ages fifteen through seventeen, listen to stories of a fabled time when Americans went to war wearing white hats, and "technical problems" didn't scrub missions. Somebody fixed the machine and the fight went on.

Ancient history, in other words.

When Earl Sheriff finished his lecture, one of the students asked him if he ever saw any of the men he had fought beside.

The custodian said there was an annual reunion of the 121st, but he had never been able to attend.

"Never could get time off from work," he said. Another problem is that his wife is an invalid.

I wondered about those students. Did they really care today how we gave Hitler hell, and what the cost of it was? Have we been on a losing streak so long they could not look at the old man in front of them and sense his pride for having a job to do, and for having done it?

Get the picture here. As the students' teacher put it, "This is still middle America. This is mostly a farm community. These are good kids. They care."

They do. I'll keep this short. What the students did was canvass the school and ask for donations. They raised $250, and they gave it to Earl Sheriff for a round-trip airplane ticket to Macon, Georgia, this week.

There he will attend the reunion of the 121st Infantry Regiment for the first time.

"Seeing all those fellows again," he said, "was always a dream of mine. Now it is coming true."

A group of high school students in 1980 have dug deep into their pockets for an old soldier who fought with our last winner.

You're always clamoring for "good" news out there. This should be a gracious dose.

## Townsend

This will probably read like a book review, but it's not. It's a story about a friend of mine who recently had a book published, a special friend more people genuinely love than just about anybody else I know.

His name is Townsend.

Yeah, he's got a first name, "James," and a middle initial, "L.," but you don't need any of those. He is "Townsend," always "Townsend," forever "Townsend."

His book is *Dear Heart* (Peachtree Publishers), and in his book Townsend takes you from Lanett, Alabama, his hometown, to any number of magic places, with numerous stops in Atlanta, a city he describes as the best city in America for "rearing a family, living in safety, and moving around without unreasonable delay."

One of the reasons so many people love Townsend so much is

because he would be optimistic with all four engines out and the tail section on fire, flying through a hurricane.

Townsend, among other things, founded *Atlanta* magazine. He edited it and nursed it, and he did the same in Cincinnati and in New Orleans and you name the town, chances are Townsend put his genius to work there at some point.

But Atlanta, how the man loves Atlanta.

In the introduction to *Dear Heart*, fellow author and friend Pat Conroy says of Townsend and what he's meant to this city:

"Atlanta, forgetful city, feisty and brawling and on the go, has not yet honored Jim Townsend, has not paused to thank the man, has not slowed down for one single act of gratitude and appreciation to the man who helped to invent the image of Atlanta.

"But when the history of Atlanta is written, and when they talk about who created the soul of this city , they will have to deal with the brilliant, mercurial, contradictory, and infinitely complex figure of Jim Townsend."

I first met Townsend in a bar. When you met Townsend a few years back, you always met him in a bar.

"Grizzard," he said to me. "I've got a story only you can do." Townsend said that to all the writers.

You didn't always get paid. Lee Walburn, now editor-in-chief of *Atlanta Weekly*, explains on the back of Townsend's new book why that never really bothered you as much as it probably should have:

"Townsend is a lovable old basset hound of an editor whose eloquent cajolery has charmed a million words from hundreds of writers—sometimes for pay, sometimes for promises. The sharing of this collection from his own jewel bag of words pays all debts."

Townsend finally whipped his boozing problem. Now he's got another bear to fight. Cancer.

Still, he's down almost every day on the seventh floor at 72 Marietta Street where *Atlanta Weekly* comes together. He edits. He writes notes. Townsend is the most eloquent note-writer who ever doodled across a scratch pad.

His book sings. There are tent revivals, twenty-fifth anniversary parties at ice cream parlors, and he explains what a "gradualist" is, and you meet H. L. Hunt and Count Alexis de Sakhnoffsky, and there is a piece about Townsend's daddy who was sharecropping cotton in west Georgia when McKinley was shot down in Buffalo.

I just want to say one more thing, and I want to say it directly to Townsend:

I read your book in one easy sitting, and I won't be satisfied until I've read more. You're beautiful, dear heart. Just beautiful.

# No Easy Way Out

We aren't, well, close, but we've had a few high times together, enough to keep us reminiscing for a couple of hours at least before we have to start telling the same stories over again.

So I was shocked when I heard the news. This man, a young man, put a .38-caliber pistol to his head. And pulled the trigger.

Say you are just trying to get somebody's attention or sympathy. You take a few pills and wind up getting your stomach pumped out in the hospital.

I'm no shrink, but I know that if you put a pistol to your head and pull the trigger, you are serious about leaving us.

It's like the man's attorney said later: "Imagine his surprise when he woke up and found out he wasn't in the Promised Land after all. He was right back here with the rest of us."

Yeah, he lived. Barely. They were already talking about where to send the remains.

I went to see him in the hospital the other night. I'm not going to mention his name. He's had enough bad publicity in his life already, and there are two children who carry his name.

"You look awful," I said to him.

"Can you believe this?" he laughed. His spirits were surprisingly high. "The last thing in the world I try to do, and I louse it up."

He spared no details.

I already knew about his divorce. Then he ran afoul of the law. Nothing big-time, but enough to bring the heat close enough to feel it.

Then, there was the lady. Stop me if you've heard this one before.

"I thought she was really special," he said.

"They've got that way of fooling us sometimes," I said.

"I just fell apart," he said. "All I could think of was I wanted out. I wanted my ticket punched."

"So what did you do, uh, wrong?" I asked. He held a finger of his right hand to his head and explained to me what the doctors had explained to him.

"They said I held the gun at an angle, so the bullet went through my right eye and out above my left eye. They said most people who shoot themselves in the head hold the gun straight, and it blows their brains out."

Above his left eye was the hole where the bullet left his head. He has lost his right eye. I made some crack about women thinking eye-patches are sexy. He is lucky he isn't blind.

I had to ask. I had to ask what it felt like to nearly die. You've read all those stories of what people saw and felt before they miraculously escaped death's clutches.

"I don't remember anything," he said. "There was a thud in my head after I pulled the trigger, and then, two days later, I woke up and I didn't know if I was in heaven or hell. I just knew I had an awful headache and there were tubes all over me."

There was something else I had to ask. I wanted to know if he was happy he had missed the obit page after all his efforts to make it there.

"I tried to get out, and I didn't make it," he answered.

He is no manner of a poet, and I had never seen sensitivity in him before. But he had something he wanted me to read. On a yellow sheet he had scribbled out the following words:

*I am an incurable romantic. I believe in hopes, dreams, and decency. I believe in love, tenderness, kindness, and family. I believe in mankind. But I must never let my happiness depend entirely on another person's thoughts, whims, or demands. Nor can I forget the value of honesty, the harshness at times of reality, and warmth of life itself, nor the need for love.*

Nice thoughts. I got up to leave.

"If you write something in the paper about this," said the man, "will you do me one favor?"

"Sure. What?"

"Tell anybody who's thinking of doing what I did not to do it. It's not the easy way out after all."

# Dark Eyes

It's an old story. She was seventeen at the time. She's more than twice that now, but still dark-eyed and beautiful. The first time I saw her, half of my life ago, she nearly took my breath.

It was a small town in the hills, and her mother taught in the little high school. Her father split when she was a baby. Her mother never remarried. There were no more children.

Her mother raised her on grace and good manners.

"Mama," she would say, laughing, "Mama always told me to act like she was looking over my shoulder. I always knew that, somehow, she was."

The child grew to be a beauty, and also a scholar. Besides that, she sang in church and visited the old people.

The boys flocked around her and vied for even her slightest attention. Those were simpler times.

She conquered high school in a matter of days. Cheerleader, clubs, a dozen handsome fellows already left in her wake by her junior year.

She was perfect. Life was perfect. Nothing could go wrong.

Something went wrong. Forget about a drug, booze, or sex angle here, however. This was the early sixties, small town, and Homecoming Night at the high school stadium.

She was one of the finalists, and she would win, of course, because she was the most popular girl in school. The homecoming queen would be chosen by ballot of the student body, the results to be announced at half time.

She was dazzling that night, a girl-child on the fine edge of womanhood.

The results were announced. She won. Her mother beamed; she had done her best under some tough circumstances.

There was another family in the town that was THE family

99

in town. If you worked in town, normally you worked for THE family. They lived in the big house with shade trees framing the drive up to the front door.

And there was a daughter in the family, too, the same age as dark-eyes, and she was a member of the Homecoming Court that night, too.

When the name of the queen was announced, the mother of the loser stormed school officials and demanded that the ballots be re-counted. Don't forget, THE family gave money for the new gymnasium and bought uniforms for the band.

The ballots were recounted. At the end of the game, there was a simple announcement. There had been a mistake. There was a new homecoming queen.

They made dark-eyes give back her crown and her roses.

"I thought I would die," she said. "And I think I would have if it hadn't been for Mama. The embarrassment was incredible. Mama said, 'Go back to school, face whatever comes. If you run from this, it could change your entire life.'"

She didn't run. She went back to school. And when it was her time, she caught a bus out of town and never looked back.

We met again by chance the other day. I didn't mention the story, and neither did she. She's been a resounding success. The lady has guts.

I do wish I knew whatever happened to Miss Homecoming, though. I hope she got fat.

# •Eating Liver And Other Sins

One thing that has always puzzled me: every time I write a column in which I mention God, at least five people write me a letter and threaten to kill me....

# Preacher Jokes

We had the minister over for dinner the other evening, and I think this all is a part of my wife's grand plan to civilize me. Next, she probably will want me to start sleeping in pajamas. Cowboys don't sleep in pajamas, but how could a woman know that?

Anyway, back to the minister coming to dinner. I had all sorts of rules I was to follow:

- You can have a beer or two, she said, but don't get out of your mind and start wanting to sing Maurice Williams and the Zodiacs songs like you do when it's just a regular party with your weirdo friends.
- And above all, don't tell any of your preacher jokes.

My wife was very emphatic about that last rule because she knows I enjoy telling jokes about preachers.

I don't know how I got started collecting jokes about ministers, but I have what must be hundreds in my repertoire, most of which are entirely within the bounds of good taste. You even can tell them at a Rotary Club luncheon.

I have short preacher jokes:

How do you tell the difference between a Northern Baptist preacher and a Southern Baptist preacher?

A Northern Baptist preacher will tell you there ain't no hell. A Southern Baptist preacher will tell you, The hell there ain't!

(For what they pay you to tell jokes at a Rotary Club luncheon, it does just fine.)

I also have long preacher jokes:

Once there was this small town where the Methodist preacher and the Baptist preacher, both of whom were quite young, rode bicycles. One Sunday morning the Methodist preacher was riding his bicycle to church and he spotted the Baptist preacher who was on foot.

"Where is your bicycle, brother?" the Methodist preacher asked.

"My heart is heavy," replied the Baptist preacher, "I think a member of my congregation has stolen it."

The Methodist preacher was appalled. "I think I can help you," he said "When you're in the pulpit this morning, preach on the Ten Commandments. And when you come to 'Thou Shalt Not Steal,' you bear down on it, and maybe the person who stole your bicycle will get the message and be moved to return it to you."

The Baptist preacher said he would try his colleague's suggestion. Two weeks later they met again. Sure enough, the Baptist preacher had his bicycle back.

"I see my plan worked," the Methodist preacher said.

"Not exactly," said the Baptist preacher. "I did preach on the Ten Commandments, but when I got to 'Thou Shalt Not Commit Adultery,' I remembered where I left my bicycle."

That was the specific joke my wife had in mind when she told me not to tell our minister any of my preacher stories.

It was a marvelous dinner party. Just before we called it a night, the minister turned to me and said, "Hey, did you hear about the preacher who ran off with all the church's money and went to Las Vegas?"

I hadn't heard.

"Part of the money he gambled away. Part of it he spent on booze. Part of it he spent on wild women. The rest of it, he just squandered."

Amen, brother.

# •A Third Look at Love and Marriage

I get letters from people who say, "What have you got against women?" What could I possibly have against women? I've married three of them....

## Nineteen Was a Long Time Ago

She was ten the first time I saw her. So was I. She was tall and gangly and put together sort of funny.

"Is that girl going to be in our class?" asked one of my pals as we looked her over the first day of the new school year.

"I hope not," I said. The last thing we needed in the sixth grade, I reasoned, was another girl. What we needed was a good second baseman. Funny how childish priorities go.

But we both grew, she out of her gangliness. Suddenly her proportions were nearly perfect. Me, I was out of my preoccupation with baseball and into a keen interest in the opposite sex.

It was in the ninth grade that the whole blasted thing began. We went on a Sunday school hayride together, and I had never been kissed until I was kissed by her, and so, six years later, I married her.

You don't know a damn thing when you are nineteen. It should be against the law to get married when you are nineteen.

But I was spending every week missing her, and I was absolutely terrible and out of place with anybody else. I knew when I was thirteen that I would marry her, so why wait any longer?

The little church was packed. My best man, as we stood in the anteroom awaiting her arrival down the aisle, said to me:

"Look, stupid. I can have us both 500 miles away from here by morning. Just say the word."

The next morning I was in our honeymoon bed.

We lasted—I forget exactly—four years, maybe. What went wrong? I'll tell you what went wrong. We were kids, children.

I went one way in my head. She went another. It broke our mothers' hearts.

So there I am in this huge department store and people are running all around doing their Christmas shopping, and the last person I figured I would run into, I ran into.

She looked great. Still blonde and thin. Still with the fashion. We talked for fifteen minutes.

105

She lives in another city. She has a husband and two kids. She was home just for a visit.

"Tell me about your wife," she said.

I raved.

"And how is it with you?" I asked.

"He's great," she replied. "I would have never made it without him.

"You always wanted to be a writer," she went on. "Are you satisfied now?"

"What's satisfied?" I asked back. "The more you get, the more you want. It's human."

We went back and forth like that. In these situations, there is another sense that takes over. You sense what to say, and what not to say, and what to ask about, and what not to ask about.

And you sense—simultaneously—when it is time to end it. The present reality hovers.

"We were so young, weren't we?" she asked, adjusting her coat to leave.

"We didn't know a damn thing," I answered.

"I'm such a different person now. All that back then is like a dream. God, how did you put up with me? Remember the time I cried when it was my birthday and you went to a ball game? How stupid."

"That wasn't stupid. I shouldn't have gone to the ball game."

"Do you still complain about your socks not being mated exactly right?"

"Yeah. My wife goes nuts when I do that."

"There is one good thing though," she said.

"What's that?"

"Neither one of us got fat, did we?"

"No, neither one of us got fat."

I took her hand and shook it. She went one way. I went another.

# •Cats and Dogs

The more I think about it, I really don't dislike cats. It's cat-lovers who are dangerous, and that is explained in detail here. As for dogs, I've never had one to ask, "Where have you been for so long?" "Why didn't you call if you knew you were going to be late?" and "Why do we never talk?" If for no other reason, I appreciate dogs for never having asked me questions I prefer not to answer....

# The Comeback Cat

I have a very real problem at my house involving a cat. I don't like cats. I never have liked cats. I never will like cats, and that is the problem.

A cat has moved into my house. I went out of town for a couple of days. When I returned, I opened the front door, and there stood a cat—a brown cat with a speck of white on its tail.

I say "its" tail because I don't know if the cat is a boy or a girl, and I don't know how to tell the difference without resorting to some unthinkable snooping.

First, I asked the cat a question, which was an idiotic thing to do, but have you ever noticed how people are always asking their pets, especially cats, questions?

"Mommie's little darling want some din-din?" Etc.

I asked the cat, "How did you get inside my house?"

The doors had been locked. The windows were secure. Maybe the cat came down the chimney?

"Did you come down the chimney?" I asked the cat.

I did it again. I asked a dumb animal a question. What do you do next, stupid, suggest a couple of games of backgammon?

I shooed the cat out of my house, and so much for my cat problem.

Hardly. The next morning, I awakened to something furry crawling around on my head. The cat was back, and the cat was in my bed. That's impossible. I had put the cat out myself, and I had locked the doors and pulled the damper down in the chimney.

"Who put you up to this?" I asked the cat, obviously no longer in control of my faculties.

I put the cat out again.

But the cat came back. Don't ask me how the cat gets into my house, but it does. I finally reached such a point of frustration that I enlisted the help of one of my neighbors, Mrs. Framingham, a worrisome old biddy who keeps a lot of cats around. I told her how the cat was driving me up a wall.

"You wouldn't hurt the little darling, would you?" Mrs. Framingham asked me.

"I wouldn't consider any permanent injuries," I responded.

"You lay one hand on that cat, and I'll break both your arms," said Mrs. Framingham, who had a typical cat-lover's attitude: Be kind to animals, or I'll break your nose.

"Why not give the poor little creature a chance?" she went on. "It obviously likes you, and it needs a home. Why not just accept it?"

No way. Cats are sneaky—and try to get a cat to roll over and play dead or chase a stick or do all the neat things a dog will do.

Cats think they are above that. Plus, I don't want a pet that bathes more often than I do.

"Shush," said Mrs. Framingham. "Give the poor dear two weeks. In two weeks you will love it. The two of you will be inseparable. That's the beauty of cats. They grow on you."

I gave the cat two weeks. I still don't want a cat. Besides, while I was typing this, I thought of an obvious solution to the problem.

All I have to do is make the cat feel unwanted. No rough stuff, just a few subtle hints that no purring, meowing little pest is going to get the best of me, no matter what the old bat down the street says.

You don't think I mean it? From now on, daddy's little precious is going to have to sleep in its own room. And our trip to the basketball game next week is definitely off.


# Pet Killer

You have to know basset hounds to love them. I have known and loved two. I lost one in a custody battle. The other, who is three months old, lives in my house now. The dog's name is Barney. Soon he will be the size, and shape, of a canoe.

Somebody else who owns a basset hound was telling me, "They're awful dogs, really. They bark too much, they get their ears in their food and then they get their ears on everything in the house, they won't mind, and they shed all over your furniture.

"But you take one look at those big, sad eyes and you're hooked."

I know the feeling. So do Tom and Diana Thorington of Atlanta.

They have a basset hound. His name is Lance. He's two years old and he has national champions on both sides of his family. (If you really love a dog, it doesn't matter if his pedigree is more impressive than your own.)

A couple of weeks ago the Thoringtons took Lance when they went to an afternoon party at a friend's house. The friend has a large lot, so they let Lance out to play with the friend's dog, a mutt. Basset hounds are not snooty.

Sometime later the people at the party heard shots being fired across the way at a neighbor's house. The host of the party and the neighbor were not close friends. Soon you will see why.

The host and Tom Thorington left the party to see what the shooting was about. They saw the neighbor firing away at Lance and the mutt.

When they reached the man, the mutt was already dead. They didn't see Lance.

"Did you shoot my dog?" Tom Thorington screamed at the man.

"Shot two of 'em," the man replied, laughing.

"You are a rotten, no-good son of a bitch," said Tom Thorington, who was being nice.

The man put his rifle, a .22, to Tom Thorington's chest.

"I think I'll shoot you next," he said.

Tom and his friend started to walk away.

"I'll shoot you in the back," said the man.

Tom and his friend kept walking. They got lucky. Crazy with the rifle didn't shoot.

Tom began calling to Lance. A couple of minutes later he heard a muffled sound from the weeds. It was Lance, with four bullets in his throat. And more, all over his body. There were even bullet holes in Lance's long, floppy ears.

"He was shot at least *ten* times," Diana Thorington told me later. "Can you imagine somebody sighting down on a basset hound TEN times?"

I've never heard of a blacker heart.

The Thoringtons rushed Lance to the local vet.

"The vet told us to forget it," said Diana. "He said there was no way Lance would make it. But we begged him to try. We love that dog so much."

Another dog, named Rip, gave some blood, and a miracle happened. Lance lived.

Okay, some nut shoots your dog and then threatens to shoot you. What do you do about it?

"We went to the police," said Diana Thorington, "but they said there was nothing much they could do. The laws about shooting dogs are pretty weak. The police said if we filed charges it would just mean a big hassle, and probably nothing much would come of it. The man was on his own property."

It is not written that life must necessarily be fair. So the Thoringtons' friend's dog is dead, and the Thoringtons' basset hound, with a little help from his friend, barely made it, and el sicko with the gun is still off his leash.

It is written, however, that a creep who would kill one family pet and then pull a trigger ten times on what is one of God's most loving creatures will, sooner or later, get his.

Every dog has his day, so to speak. Knowing that, I rest a little easier. Not much, but a little.

# • Special Occasions

The holidays. They bring out the best and the worst in people. April 15 is not a holiday, of course, but it should be. It brings out the most in people. . . .

The response to this plea for help for Betty Hubbard was incredible. She and her son got their kitchen table and much more. There is bad in the world and, sometimes, it seems to scream out to be noticed. But there is much good, too, and Christmas brings it forth in gushes.

# Double-Dose of Hard Times

Betty Hubbard sat on what was a piece of lawn furniture before some-body bent the frame. Betty's son, Joey, who is fifteen, sat on the floor. I took one of Betty's two chairs. A second visitor sat in the other chair.

Betty Hubbard talked about her life. I caught myself looking away to avoid her eyes when she cried.

"I never thought I would come to anything like this," she said. "We ain't got a thing."

She is fifty. She looks older. She's been a "widow woman" for ten years. She has an older son who she says is a "bad influence" on young Joey.

She moved to Atlanta from neighboring Rockdale County to look for a fresh start for her and the boy.

She has asthma. She is unemployed. She and Joey live in a hole of an apartment near Grant Park.

"I apologize for the way this place looks," Betty said. "Me and Joey got out a bucket of water and scrubbed these floors, but it didn't do no good."

We are seated in the living room. There is a small table near the door. On the table are pictures of Betty's sons. Between the two chairs is a locker. There is a small lamp on the locker. It is the only light in the house.

There is no table in the kitchen. There are two bedrooms in the apartment, but only one bed.

"Joey has to sleep with me," said Betty Hubbard. "A lot of folks might have something to say about that, but if he don't sleep with me, then he has to sleep on the floor. I ain't lettin' my baby sleep on no floor. He's all I got."

The sky is gray, the weather is cold. For the first two weeks Betty and Joey were in the apartment, they did not have the money to have the gas and power turned on. They huddled under blankets and burned candles.

Betty gets four hundred dollars a month in welfare payments. She hands over $220 for the apartment. She's being robbed. She borrowed from her landlord to put down the deposits for the gas and power.

"We had a home once," Betty goes on, breaking into tears, "but it got away from me. It's hard for a widow woman and two boys."

There was a silence in the room.

"I don't lie to my doctor, so I won't lie to you," Betty Hubbard continued. "We've all done some drinking. Me, and both the boys. All it done was cause fighting and misunderstanding. But there were times we didn't have nothing to eat. Where there ain't nothing to eat and somebody comes around with a drink, you just can't help but take it."

Betty Hubbard's apartment is a curse. Crumpled magazines and newspapers on the floor. Towels over the windows. Something caught my eye hanging on the wall, a baby's Christmas stocking marked "Joey," and a Christmas scene torn from a calendar. Christmas finds the darndest places.

Hard times come in different degrees. Betty and her boy Joey have caught a double-dose. They're flat busted and it's Christmas Eve. They don't ask much:

- Some pants for Joey. He has only one pair. The is thirty in the waist and thirty length.
- Some shoes for Betty. Her only pair are worn moccasins.
- A small bed for Joey. And something where the two of them could sit down for a meal.
- Food. They ate sardines and soda crackers for Thanksgiving.
- An old television. "A boy naturally wants a television, said Betty Hubbard. "When I get back on my feet, that's the first thing I'm going to do, get my boy a television."
- Employment. Betty, with her asthma, is limited. She says she is good with children and once worked in a nursery. Joey is strong.

You hear these stories every Christmas. And you can't help everybody. And there are probably people even more deserving than Betty and Joey Hubbard, and, besides, we've got our own families to take care of.

But when the party is over and the wrappings are off the gifts, and Friday brings back reality, Betty and Joey still won't have a kitchen table.

They Tore Out My Heart and Stomped That Sucker Flat *documents Grizzard's heart troubles, both literal and figurative. The title and dedication of* They Tore Out My Heart *says it all; Lewis Grizzard dedicates this, his first original narrative book, to several doctors and nurses of the cardiovascular section of Emory University Hospital. Grizzard takes the reader from the discovery of his heart condition, called aortic insufficiency, through the valve replacement surgery and his recovery. He also compares and contrasts the fixable, physical heart with its romantic, less tangible counterpart. In the process, Grizzard reveals what he feared the most when he confronted death: not being able to relive those experiences of everyday life that he had accepted as commonplace. The remembrances the surgery ordeal sparks touch on the people and experiences Grizzard cherished most, and allow the reader a very special glance into Grizzard's more private memories.*

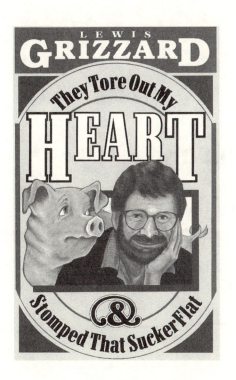

**LEWIS GRIZZARD**

They Tore Out My

# HEART

& Stomped That Sucker Flat

1982

# •The Hog and I

"How the hog, one of God's most interesting creations, got involved in the surgery on my heart is a long story. . . ."

How the hog, one of God's most interesting creations, got involved in the surgery on my heart is a long story. After we had set a date for my appointment with the man with the knife, the doctors sat me down to discuss one remaining question.

We know we want to put in a new aortic valve in your heart, they said, but we don't know which type.

Which type? You mean this is like going into Baskin-Robbins and trying to decide between almond toffee and chocolate marshmallow? I wouldn't know an aortic valve if it walked up and bit me on the leg. What is this business with types?

I had a feeling when the discussion began that this little matter wouldn't be simple. It wasn't. I will attempt to decipher for you what the doctors attempted to explain to me.

In the first place, valve replacement isn't something that has been going on for years as my senior doctor had explained when I was trying to weasel my way out of having the operation in the first place.

Twenty-five years ago, the man had said, they would have put me on some pills and then we would have all sat around and waited for my heart to get the size of my head, which would have been about the time it would have stopped beating, a situation terribly hazardous to one's health.

Finally, somebody did invent an artificial heart valve and procedures whereby it could be inserted in place of the one the patient came with. The first valves were mechanical and were constructed of totally artificial materials, such as plastic.

They were better than no replacement valves at all, but there were problems. Patients with the mechanical valves faced the possibility of such complications as blood-clotting, which could lead to such unpleasant situations as strokes. So, it was necessary for patients with mechanical valves to take anticoagulants to avoid the clotting, but thin blood isn't such a terrific idea, either. The biggest plus for mechanical valves was they were durable.

There obviously have been improvements in mechanical valves over the ensuing years, but the dangers of clotting and stroke and the

119

matter of taking blood thinners indefinitely have remained.

"Little boogers will last just about forever," one of my doctors said, "but if we put one of those in you, I'd hate to see you dragging a foot around because of a stroke somewhere down the road."

I can understand doctors when they talk like that. Dragging a foot around isn't exactly my style.

Fortunately, I had another choice. A decade or so ago, researchers had the bright idea of attempting to develop a valve made from animal tissue. In the beginning, I suppose they tried taking valves from all sorts of animals and testing them for use in the human heart.

I would have started with elephants. When is the last time you've heard of an elephant dropping dead with a heart attack? I would have stayed away from nervous animals like those monkeys you see at the zoo who can't sit still and make those awful screeching noises.

I probably would have never thought of hogs. Hogs make all sorts of noises, too, like they're having trouble breathing; they don't get out of the mud or away from the food trough long enough to get any exercise; and then there is the matter of their smell.

When I was growing up in Coweta County, Georgia, a lot of people raised hogs. You could always tell which of your classmates had hogs at their house by noticing if there were empty seats around them in the classroom.

The Rainwaters raised hogs. Nobody would ever take a seat next to a Rainwater child in school because it was difficult to pay attention to what was the average per annum rainfall in Ethiopia and fight off the distinct odor of swine at the same time. Claude Rainwater, who was in my class, even had a pet hog, which he occasionally rode to school. The hog's name was Lamar. Claude would tie Lamar to a small tree in the school yard and Lamar would wait patiently until school was out and then Claude would ride him home again.

One day, Claude came to school without Lamar. He was in tears.

"What's the matter, Claude?" the teacher asked him.

"It's my pet hog," said Claude. "Daddy won't let me ride him to school anymore."

"Why is that?" the teacher continued.

"Daddy said he was going to have puppies."

Perhaps they should have told us less about the rainfall in Ethiopia in those days and spent at least a little time on why hogs don't have puppies, and even if one did, why it certainly shouldn't be named Lamar.

I was very surprised when my doctors told me my other choice for a new valve was one that would be taken from a hog. Only they didn't say "hog valve," they said "porcine valve," which is the same thing. Hog. Porcine. They both grunt and will eat things the dogs won't touch.

The advantage a valve taken from a hog would have over a mechanical valve, they explained, was the hog valve reduced the possibility of dangerous clotting and also required no blood thinners. Hog valves and human valves, they said, were very much alike.

I waited for the catch. The catch, they said, was the question of the durability of the animal tissue valve.

"It won't last as long as a mechanical valve?" I asked.

"How many fifty-year-old hogs do you know?" was the answer.

Specifically, the porcine valves have been in use for something like ten years, and those implanted in the beginning have exhibited a tendency to wear out.

"What happens if one wears out?" I asked further.

"A second operation for a new one."

I did some quick arithmetic. I'm thirty-five. I plan to live out my years. I'll take seventy-five and call it even.

At one operation to put in a new valve every ten years, that's four operations to go. At that rate, I could wipe out a small hog farm like the Rainwaters' by myself.

Plus, there was the consideration of something out of a hog being placed inside my body. I mentioned some of the things that worried me about hogs, their snorting and labored breathing, their diet, their acute laziness, and their smell.

Despite all that, however, I have always had a voracious appetite for barbecue and even fancy myself as quite an expert on the subject. What would happen to me with hog in my heart?

Every time I'd pass a barbecue restaurant, my eyes would fill with tears?

Barbecue. My thoughts raced back to the integral part it has played in my life.

There was the annual Fourth of July Barbecue in my hometown. The churches went in together and bought some hogs and then the menfolk would sit up all night before the Fourth and barbecue the hogs over hickory smoke in an open pit, which doesn't take a great deal of work once the hogs are cooking, so the menfolk had a lot of time to sit around and talk, mostly about the Bible.

They would talk Revelation for a time, which always spooked me, and then they would get along to something like Deuteronomy.

The Fourth of July Barbecue drew people from as far away as Newnan, LaGrange, and Hogansville. One year, a man from North Carolina was passing through and stopped in to partake.

He asked for the cole slaw.

"What for?" somebody asked. "There's plenty of stew and light bread."

"I want to put it on my barbecue," the man from North Carolina said.

I learned my first rule about barbecue that day. You don't put cole slaw on it. I think that's in Deuteronomy somewhere.

Somebody pulled a knife on the man and he got back in his car and went back to North Carolina.

After I left home, I roamed freely about other parts of the country, and I came to understand several truths about barbecue:

- The best barbecue is served in the state of Georgia. In Texas, they barbecue beef, which isn't barbecue at all, and neither is goat, which is stringy. I wouldn't even put cole slaw on barbecued goat out of respect for the cole slaw.
- The best barbecue is found in family-run operations. Harold Hembree, who runs Harold's Barbecue in Atlanta, can't even count the number of cousins and nieces and nephews working for him. There are three generations of Sprayberrys cooking and serving at Sprayberry's in Newnan, Georgia. Sweat's is a family operation in Soperton, Georgia, and it was Jim Brewer's father-in-law who first started Fresh-Air in Jackson, Georgia, fifty-one years ago when he served off a sawdust floor. "When it's a family working together," says Jim Brewer, "things get done right."
- If there are religious posters on the wall, you can usually count on the barbecue's being good. Harold's is a perfect example.
- Good barbecue restaurants rarely serve beer, as good as beer is with barbecue. "Mama won't allow it here," is why Harold Hembree doesn't serve beer at his place. "You'll lose your family trade," says Jim Brewer of Fresh-Air.

- If a restaurant specializes in something besides barbecue, the barbecue probably won't be any good. You can serve other things, just don't brag on it. Jack Sweat in Soperton is still amazed at the time a family of Yankees headed for Florida stopped by his place and ordered fried shrimp.
- Georgia barbecue restaurants are careful what kind of bread they serve with their meat. Normally, it's thin buns for sandwiches, and white bread for plates. Harold's toasts white bread over an open flame for sandwiches and serves cracklin' cornbread with its plates. I think Harold will go to heaven for his cracklin' cornbread.
- Brunswick stew is too complicated to get into. Everybody has a different idea about how it should be cooked and what it should contain. "We even get 'em who complain unless the stew's been cooked in a hog's head," says Jim Brewer.
- Sauce: Ditto. In Georgia alone there are hundreds of varieties of sauces. If the meat is good, the sauce will be, too.
- It is important to put up a sign in a barbecue restaurant that says "No Shoes. No Shirt. No Service." That will add class to the place by keeping out people from Texas and North Carolina.

My doctors assured me the installation of a porcine valve into my heart would have no effect upon my taste and desire and enjoyment of good barbecue.

"You might have some other problems, though," said one.

"What's that?" I asked.

"You might want to go out and root for truffles occasionally," he laughed.

"And you might crave watermelon rinds and corncobs," said another.

"What you really have to watch," a third chimed in, "is every afternoon about four o'clock, you might get this strange desire to go out and make love in the mud."

Doctors stay inside too much, I think.

Aside from the questions of the durability of the valves and the barbecue thing, there were a couple of other concerns.

I wondered where they kept the hogs who were kind enough to donate their valves for people in my condition.

You know the outrage we have over the slaughter of baby seals. They go out and hit those baby seals with a lead pipe or something, and people are up in the air about that everywhere.

I was afraid they kept the hogs in a pen out behind the hospital. I've been prepared for surgery and the doctor says to an orderly, "Leon, go out to the hog pen and get me a valve."

Leon goes out to the hog pen with a two-by-four and whomps a hog on the head and they take out his valve.

The doctors assured me nothing like that took place, which was a relief. Hogs have feelings, too, I expect.

I considered the question of porcine versus mechanical valve for about a minute.

MECHANICAL: I couldn't get the idea of dragging a leg very far out of my mind.

PORCINE: So it wears out in ten years. At least I wouldn't have to take the blood thinners and worry about a stroke. And medical science moves so swiftly. In ten years, who knows? Maybe they would come up with a solution where you just take a pill.

There was just that one other thing I wanted to know after the decision was made to install the porcine valve.

"It's just a little thing," I said.

"Shoot," said one of the doctors.

"Do the pigs that give up their valves have names?" The doctor said he would check.

"Do you have a preference of a name for your donor?" he asked.

"Not really," I answered. "Just as long as it isn't Lamar."

# • Adventures in ICU

"No incisions were actually made into the muscle of my heart. The work was done on the outside where the valve meets the aorta. I did not then undergo 'open heart surgery' and neither do most other heart surgery patients.... 'Open heart surgery' is what the guy down the street thinks you had. So let him think that. Its sounds more exotic than just heart surgery, anyway."

The head nurse came into the room at ten o'clock and asked everyone to leave. Everyone except me, of course. This was the part of the pre-surgery period I had dreaded the most. I said my good-byes.

"You're sure about your red coat?" asked my friend, the Shriner.

"Positive," I said.

My stepfather was there. He's a good man who married my mother when I was ten and who has looked after her all these years and who is solid in situations like these. My mother's own health problems had kept her from being with me.

"Tell Mother I love her," I said to my stepfather.

"I'll tell her," he said.

We shook hands. If I had it all to do over again, I would have hugged his neck.

I kissed my wife. I wanted to say something poetic, like if I didn't make it, I'd meet her just beyond the moon. I heard that line in a Tex Ritter song, believe it or not.

All I could say to her was, "Thanks for bringing the chili dogs." I guess I'm no Tex Ritter.

The nurse gave me another sleeping pill and turned out my light. It was dark. I was alone. The buses had stopped running at ten. I prayed one last time. All I could do now was let the drugs take my dreams and what was left of my fear.

At six in the morning, another nurse brought me out of what had actually been a restful sleep with a gentle tug on my arm. She even had the morning newspaper. I read the sports section first. North Carolina was storming toward the collegiate basketball championship. There was a story about how lousy the Chicago Cubs were looking in spring practice.

That reminded me to look in my little bag I had brought with me from home. Something else I put in there I forgot to mention. I put in my lucky Chicago Cubs baseball cap I bought one day when I lived in Chicago and used to walk up to Addison and Clark Streets to Wrigley Field to watch the Cubs mostly lose.

The reason I figure a Chicago Cubs baseball cap is lucky is this: The Cubs haven't won a pennant since 1945. Season after season, they are a terrible disappointment to their followers. Yet, no Cub has ever been seriously injured by an irate fan, which is a minor miracle. Maybe, I concluded, it was the caps that kept the players from harm.

I put on my Cubs cap while the nurse scurried around my bed, taking my temperature and checking my blood pressure.

"What are you doing with that hat on?" she asked.

"It's not a hat," I replied. "It's a cap. Don't you know anything about baseball?"

"I don't care what it is," the nurse replied, "but you'll have to take it off when we take you out."

I hadn't counted on this.

"What's wrong with me wearing a cap when you take me out?" I inquired, a bit indignantly.

"You can't wear something like that into surgery because it can't be sterilized," she said.

Once a guy sitting behind me at Wrigley Field had tried for a foul ball and spilled his beer on my cap, but other than that, it was perfectly clean.

"I'm wearing my cap," I said.

"You want another enema?" asked the nurse.

I put my cap back in my bag and went into the bathroom to take my shower.

They give you a brush and medicated soap for your pre-op shower. The soap is yellow. Actually, it's caramel colored. Actually, it was the color of that lotion they came out with years ago called "Q.T." for "quick tan." The idea was to spread it over your body and it would give you an instant tan without you ever having to set foot into the hot sun. The problem, of course, was that it was impossible to spread the lotion over your body evenly, so you wound up looking like a pinto pony.

What you are supposed to do is scrub that soap all over your body with the brush. The brush has very brittle teeth, and your body, having been shaved the night before, is very tender. When I finished my shower, my body felt like the entire Chicago Cubs infield had just walked across it wearing their cleats.

There was something that had been worrying me about this

particular moment. I did not relish the idea of being conscious when they rolled me into the operating room. I didn't want to see it. I didn't want to see the table. I didn't want to see the operating team. I didn't want to see the table of instruments. I was also afraid they might have the little pig in there who was donating the valve. I didn't want to come face to face with the pig, either.

No problem. The nurse gave me another Valium, a whammo dosage. I began to drift off. I barely remember what came next. What came next was a shot in my rear to take me even farther out.

I have no recollection whatsoever of leaving my hospital room. As a matter of fact, I have no recollection whatsoever of the next eight or so hours. I can reconstruct it here only through later conversations with those involved in my operation and in my immediate postoperative care.

At 6:45 A.M., they wheeled me out of my hospital room toward the surgical unit. I was carrying on, they said, but nobody was exactly certain what I was carrying on about. Everything was normal so far.

Before entering the operating room, I was taken to what is called a holding room. It was 7:15. Further preparation was made for the surgery. EKG leads were put into place. Small lines were placed in various arteries for measuring pressures.

At 8 A.M., I was taken into the operation room. More lines and tubes. One anesthetic ended my senseless carrying-on and put me even farther out. Another blocked nerves in order to relax my body. More tubes, including the one tube I had worried about the most. The one to my bladder.

"We always wait until the patient is all the way under before we put in that catheter," a doctor told me later. I would like to go on record as thanking the medical profession for that concession to the comfort of their patients.

There were eight other people in the room besides the one sound asleep with the bladder catheter in him. Three on the surgical team, two anesthesiologists, a nurse assisting, a nurse circulating, and two to run the heart-lung machine.

My body was covered with sterile drapes. The lines and tubes were in place. The surgeon took his scalpel and made the initial incision into my skin. He started just below the base of my neck and went just below my sternum, four inches above my navel. Something to know about having heart surgery. Very little muscle tissue is cut when the incision is made. That cuts down on painful muscle spasms that cause so much discomfort following surgery to other parts of the body.

This is the part that gives me the creeps: After the skin incision is made, the surgeon takes in hand what is known as a Stryker saw. It is an oscillating saw that cuts through the breastbone. I was told it cuts through the bone very cleanly and doesn't make a lot of noise, so do not think about the movie, *The Texas Chain Saw Massacre*, as you read this.

Once they had cut through my breastbone, a chest retractor was used to open a large area in my chest in order to give the surgeons room to work. My ribs buckled in the process. This creates a great deal of discomfort following surgery, but at least the doctors have room to use both hands.

Then came the stickiest part of the procedure. The reason it is possible to make necessary repairs to the heart today, is the development of the heart-lung machine. They explained to me the details of how it works, but here is about all I understood.

The heart must be stopped so the surgeon can do his work. The heart is stopped by cooling it. The entire body of the patient is cooled to twenty-eight degrees centigrade (eighty-two, Fahrenheit), as a matter of fact, which reduces the metabolism of the heart and also reduces the amount of oxygen it needs, a safeguard against further damage to the heart muscle during the surgery.

A tube is inserted into the aorta on the left side of the heart, and then two more tubes are inserted into the right side. Blood then actually bypasses the heart through the tubes and flows into the heart-lung machine, which oxygenates it and filters it and circulates it throughout the body.

The heart is not beating. It is clear of blood. But the surgeon is able to work on a live patient because of that marvelous machine that is taking the place of the patient's heart and lungs.

A clamp was placed on my aorta, the artery leading from the left ventricle of my heart. My aorta was then opened and the surgeons looked in at the valve for the first time.

The leaflets of my valve, I was told later, were elongated and thin from overwork and were falling back into my heart chamber.

The leaflets of my original valve were taken out. Fifteen sutures went in to hold the new valve, which had arrived in the operating room without its original owner, I was assured later.

I received a twenty-seven millimeter, Carpentier tissue valve, produced by American Edwards Laboratories, Model No. 2625, Serial No. AB0574. (I never did get the hog's name.) The valve I received was comparatively large. The larger the better. The problem with tissue valves is if and when they begin to deteriorate, they also begin to shrink. Larger valves have farther to shrink before there is trouble and blood leakage begins all over again.

One other note. No incisions were actually made into the muscle of my heart. The work was done on the outside where the valve meets the aorta. I did not then undergo "open heart surgery" and neither do most other heart surgery patients. Coronary bypass surgery, the most common sort of heart surgery today, for instance, requires no entrance into the heart chamber itself. "Open heart surgery" is what the guy down the street always thinks you had. So let him think that. It sounds more exotic than just heart surgery, anyway.

Once the valve is in place, the heart is warmed again and all electrical activity restarts. The patient comes off the bypass of the heart-lung machine, the most critical period is over. What is left to do is put his chest back together again.

The sternum is closed with heavy stainless steel wire that grows into the core of the bone. This causes no pain afterwards, but when you have chest X-rays taken later, it looks like you swallowed a box of paper clips.

As far as putting the skin back together, I got lucky. My surgeon practices a method whereby the sutures run underneath the skin surface so your chest doesn't look like a football. My scar, as a matter of fact, looks like I was stealing eggs and the chicken scratched me. Nobody who sees my scar is the slightest bit repulsed by its appearance, not even strangers I stop on the street.

The actual procedure of opening my chest, diverting my blood to the heart-lung machine, replacing my valve, taking me off bypass, and closing my chest again took fifty-one minutes.

There were no problems. No complications. Damn good surgical team.

There is nothing for family and friends to do but wait. The hospital was kind enough to provide a private waiting area. They wouldn't allow the two witch doctors in, however. I paid two witch doctors fifty bucks each to dance and chase away any evil heart-surgery spirits that might have been lurking within a twenty-five-mile radius of DeKalb County, Georgia. They also make the girls' drum and bugle corps I had hired wait in the parking lot. They were to hit it when word came I had survived the operation. You cover all the bases in a situation like this.

My senior cardiologist, a learned and kind and gentle man, kept those who love me most posted on my progress.

He told them when I went on the bypass machine. He told them when the surgery was over. I understand the subsequent celebration set no records, but the girls' drum and bugle corps was well into their third number in the parking lot before somebody called the cops.

My secretary waited in my office. She was given word the surgery had been a success. She was to pass it on to the thousands who would be calling in.

I asked her later how many people actually called.

"Two," she said.

"Two thousand?"

"No, two, period. One was from an old friend calling long distance. He wanted to know if you had lived."

"And what did you tell him?"

"I told him you were alive, but you didn't know it yet."

"Who else called?"

"The captain of your league tennis team."

"What did he say?"

"Well, after I told him you were okay, he said, 'Now what in the hell am I going to do with a dozen black armbands?' "

After the surgery was completed, I was taken to the Coronary Intensive Care Unit where a tube was inserted in my throat and down into my lungs. This is called a respirator tube. It does your breathing for you until your lungs can shake off the effects of the anesthetic and the effect of inactivity while the patient is on the heart-lung machine. It is during this period the lungs fill with fluids.

My family and friends were allowed into my room in the Intensive Care Unit soon after I arrived there.

"I thought you were dead," my wife told me later.

"You were cold and white as a sheet," said my stepfather.

131

"I've seen you look worse only one other time," said one of my friends.

When I had the Asian flu and was in bed for a week?

"No, the morning after you drank the bottle of tequila at the beach and ate three dozen raw oysters and we found you asleep with your head in the john."

I remember that. I was so sick I wanted to drown myself, but I knew I could never make it to the ocean, so I tried the nearest available water source.

Let's go back to the respirator tube. They had told me about the respirator tube the day before my surgery.

"We will put in a respirator tube following the surgery. When you first awaken, there will be some discomfort. We will have to restrain your arms because some patients have been known to attempt to remove their respirator tubes."

The first thing I did when I regained consciousness following my surgery was to attempt to remove my respirator tube. There's that medical understatement again. "Some discomfort." Sheer terror.

I opened my eyes and I tried to do something very simple like take a breath. I couldn't take a breath. I tried to take another breath. Nothing. I panicked. I was very much aware of the respirator tube. This, I reasoned, was what was responsible for my inability to breathe.

I tried to reach to my mouth and pull the respirator tube out of my body and throw it at whomever was responsible for putting it there. I had forgotten the part about my arms being restrained.

I looked around me. One of my friends was standing to the left of me. Thank God, I thought. He will get this thing out of my throat so I can breathe. I tried to say, "Get this thing out of my throat so I can breathe!" to my friend.

Something else they had told me that I had forgotten. You can't talk with a respirator tube in your throat because they shove it down through your voice box. I made a mental note to discuss this with my doctors later, in the event I managed to somehow survive this obvious attempt to kill me. Somebody was going to by-God pay for this trick.

Then I remembered they had also told me if I wanted to communicate during the time the respirator tube was in my throat, there would be a tablet and pencil near my right hand and I could write out what I wanted to say.

I felt for the tablet and pencil. Nothing. I had one last chance. I reached my right hand as high as it would reach with the straps around my arm and I tried to write out certain words in the air.

"Look," said my friend at my left, "he's trying to tell us something."

"What do you think he's trying to say?" asked my wife, who was standing nearby.

"I think he's trying to say hello."

"How cute," said my wife.

I wasn't trying to say hello. I was trying to say I had about eight seconds to live and don't just stand there like a couple of raw oysters, get this blessed tube out of my throat.

Finally a nurse got the message.

"He doesn't think he can breathe," she said. "It happens to everybody."

She peered over my bed and looked squarely into my fear-stricken eyes.

"Just relax," she said. "The tube is doing your breathing."

I reached my hand up again and tried to write, "You wouldn't kid me, would you?" in the air.

"He'll go back to sleep in a minute," I heard the nurse say.

Some patients keep the tube longer than others. Some patients' lungs clear up more quickly than others. If a patient is a smoker, he can keep the tube down his throat for twenty-four hours or more. On May 10, 1980, I had given up smoking.

When I awakened for the second time, four or five hours later, the tube was out of my throat and I could breathe on my own. I couldn't reach down there and pull in a big gulp of air because of all the diddling around that had been done in my chest, but what little breath I could manage never felt better.

I vividly recall the thought I had at this marvelous moment: They ought to burn every tobacco field still standing.

# •Tubes

"There are seven places on the human body where a tube may be inserted without making a new hole. (I'll wait a second while you count.) I don't think God had any intention for anybody to go sticking tubes, or anything else, in at least a couple of these holes, but they stick tubes there anyway when they operate on your heart."

**F**rankly I would like to end any further discussion of tubes at this point, but tubes are what surgery is all about, especially after the patient reaches the Intensive Care Unit where the tubes begin to come out.

There are seven places on the human body where a tube may be inserted without making a new hole. (I'll wait a second while you count.) I don't think God had any intention for anybody to go sticking tubes, or anything else, in at least a couple of those holes, but they stick tubes there anyway when they operate on your heart.

I'm not certain the exact number of tubes they eventually stick in you before, during, and after heart surgery, but it is considerably more than seven, which means they have to make some new holes. Just north of your navel, they make two, one to the east and one to the west, and that's where your chest tubes go.

I wasn't aware of it when they made the chest tube holes in my stomach because I was under the anesthetic at that point. Nobody would have made chest tubes holes in my stomach, otherwise, because as a small boy growing up in the rural South, I learned if anybody came at you with something sharp with the intention of making new holes in you, you ran away as fast as you possibly could and called the local authorities and reported somebody was trying to cut you, which was against the law in my county unless it could be proved the victim needed cutting.

One morning after I had regained some of my senses in ICU, I was relaxing with a jar of morphine when a doctor I had never seen before walked casually into my room, whistling.

"I'm going to remove your chest tubes," he said, once he had stopped whistling.

My chest tubes, I had been told earlier, were for the purpose of drainage. Some tubes they use to put things into you. Others they use to take things out. Fully-tubed, a heart surgery patient bears a great deal of resemblance to the distributor cap of a 1956 Plymouth Fury.

It hurt. Morphine or no morphine, the removal of my chest tubes was the worst thing that happened to me during the entire experience of having heart surgery.

"You okay?" asked the doctor once he had removed the tubes.

"Get away from me," I said.

I felt like he had snatched my innards from their very holdings.

"Come back with my pancreas!" I screamed at the doctor as he left the room, whistling again. I didn't even get his tag number.

I will never forget how it felt to have my chest tubes removed. Now, every time I hear a whistling sound, I double up into a tight knot and fall on the floor and lie very still, which is a problem only when I am driving in heavy traffic and the radio station to which I am tuned tests its Emergency Alert System.

The chest tube experience did have its value, however, and that was to assure me that I had lived through the operation. You can't be dead and hurt that badly at the same time.

After the chest tube horror, I began to count the other tubes that were running in and out of my body. I started with the one in my neck. That is called a Swan-Ganz Catheter. It measures various pressures in the body. Find a pressure somewhere and somebody in a hospital is going to want to measure it, even if it means sticking a tube in your neck.

There were also needles and lines in my arms and wrists. I was being fed through one. Given a choice between eating the lunch they served my first day in the hospital and getting food from a bottle through a tube and a needle, I'd go for the bottle and the tube and the needle every time. At least there was no chewing involved.

Another line was for the morphine to kill pain. Except for when somebody wants to pull a tube out of your stomach, the pain immediately following the heart surgery is quite bearable, as long as you lie perfectly still.

There was another tube in my rectum to measure my temperature. Why the rectum is a good place to measure a person's temperature is beyond me, but at least it doesn't take a large tube to do the job, which is something for which I was quite grateful.

I also noticed some small wires that had been attached to my stomach. They were pacemaker wires. In case there arose the need to alter my heartbeat, the wires could be used to send electrical impulses to my heart. They mess your stomach up pretty good when they operate on your heart.

Then, of course, there was the bladder catheter, and we all know where they stick that. I couldn't bear to look at where they had stuck my bladder catheter.

All around me were machines with dials and screens and things making beeping noises.

"Every part of your body is being monitored," a nurse told me.

She was a very pretty nurse, with dark hair and when she walked around in my room in her snug nurse's outfit, I found myself monitoring certain parts of her body.

"Do me a favor," I said to her.

"What's that?"

"Walk past me again and let's see if the machine beeps louder."

She did and it did, and I felt quite comfortable in the assumption heart surgery hadn't affected my capacity for lust, even with the aforementioned tube the size of a small garden hose intruding in the situation.

In Intensive Care, one by one, the tubes began to come out. The chest tubes went out by the hand of the whistling doctor. The nurse took out the Swan from my neck. The lines came out of my arms and wrists. No problem.

Then, one morning the nurse pulled back the sheet and announced it was time to remove the bladder catheter.

"And you're going to do it?" I asked.

"I do this all the time," she said.

The stories she must have.

It wasn't all that bad, compared to the removal of the chest tubes. The nurse gave the tube a tug and out it came with nothing more than a slight sting. I couldn't bear to look, however.

"Everything seem to be in order?" I asked her with a slight halt in my voice.

"Little fellow's looking just fine to me," she answered.

You'd think a nurse with that much experience in such matters would have elected to use a better choice of words.

Before I left ICU, the cough lady came to see me. I don't know her official title, but she came into my room and explained that it was time I got out of bed, sat myself down in a chair and coughed.

"You need to cough up the fluids in your lungs," she said.

She helped me out of the bed to the chair. My first steps were slow. I was dizzy, for one thing. I figured I still wasn't over the chili dogs.

After I had sat down in the chair, the lady brought me a pillow and said to hold it to my chest as tightly as I could.

"This will ease some of the pain when you try to cough," she explained.

She even told me how to cough.

"Take as deep a breath as you can take and then cough several times as hard as you can. Like this..."

She took a deep breath, clutched the pillow and made a sound like somebody trying to crank a pulpwood truck on a cold morning.

"HRRRACK! HRRRACK! HRRRRACK!" went the cough lady.

I took a deep breath and squeezed the pillow to my chest. I didn't go "HRRRACK!" at all. I barely made a sound.

"You've got to try harder," said the cough lady.

I tried again, but I didn't try harder. I knew if I tried harder, it would hurt and no stupid pillows would make it stop.

The cough lady came back two or three more times and tried to get me to do a couple of hrrracks. I never did the first one.

"You don't smoke?" she asked.

"Gave it up two years ago."

"Smokers have to do a lot of coughing after their surgery. I guess you don't have any fluids left in your lungs."

"I won't tell anybody if you won't," I said.

The cough lady left and went to bother somebody else.

I was very pleased to get out of Intensive Care and back into a regular room in the coronary wing. The only thing still attached to my body that hadn't come attached in the first place were the pacemaker wires on my stomach. My first morning out of ICU another doctor I had never seen came to take those out. He carried a pair of wire snippers. He snipped this wire and then that wire.

"Dang if you're not a bleeder," he laughed.

I looked at my stomach. It was very red.

I remained as still as possible and didn't say a word while the doctor finished. You don't risk arousing a man who thinks a stomach covered with blood is funny, especially if he is packing a pair of wire snippers at the time.

My cardiologist came in and checked my heart.

"Sounds just fine," he said.

A couple of his assistants came in and they listened to my heart, too.

"Outstanding," said one.

"Couldn't be better," said the other.

My blood pressure. They checked that, too. Before the surgery, the range had been extremely wide. I even recorded a two hundred over zero at one point.

After surgery, I was one-twenty over eighty. Perfect.

I looked at my scar. I had expected it to be much worse. There would also be two small scars from the chest-tube incisions, but once the hair grew back on my chest, they would be barely visible.

There was pain when I tried to get a deep breath, but nothing I couldn't handle. The area around my collarbone and my sides were sore from the chest retractor during surgery, but that wasn't so terrible, either.

I was still a bit foggy from all the drugs, but I'd been foggier. Recall the tequila and oyster episode.

I had made it. The surgeons had plugged the leak in my heart, my blood pressure couldn't have been better, and my prior fear of being delirious with pain at this point had been a needless concern. I was in only mild discomfort.

All this presented a bit of a problem, however. You don't go through heart surgery and not expect a large portion of sympathy. If the doctors and nurses and my family and friends knew how good I really felt, they might not feel as sorry for me as I wanted them to feel, and they might not continue to wait on me hand and foot as I most certainly deserved.

I decided to do one of the things I do best in order to assure everyone involved I was in a most pitiable state. I decided to whine a lot.

I can whine with the best of them. I have different whines for different situations. There is my hangover whine.

"Ohhhhhhhhhhhhhhh, my Goooooood!" is my basic hangover whine.

"I think I am going to die," is the whine I use when I have a bad cold and I want somebody to bring my ginger ale and chicken noodle soup and a piece of carrot cake, which will cure a cold in a New York minute, as long as you can get somebody else to bring it to you.

When I really want some attention and sympathy, however, I use a whine that defies a spelling.

It's sort of "Ooooooooooh," but with some "Awwwwwwwwwww," and a kind of high-pitched "Uhhhhhhhhh" thrown in. Ever heard the sound a dog makes when you step on its tail? It's sort of like that, too, except a dog takes a little break between sounds. When I use this whine, I am steady and constant with it.

I use this whine in the dentist's chair, and I used to use it when my mother wanted me to go outside and pull weeds out of her flowers, and I tried it on a state patrolman once who had stopped me for speeding. The dentist always ignores me and so did the heartless state patrolman, but I still haven't pulled the first weed out of my mother's flower garden.

"How do you feel?" my wife asked me the first afternoon I was out of ICU.

I put the big whine on her.

"Bless your heart," she said.

A couple of guys from my tennis team came in to see me.

"How are you feeling?" one asked.

I let go a dandy.

"Let's get out of here," said the other. "He's giving me the creeps."

You would figure nurses would know better than to go for whining. They don't. There was one nurse from ICU who had been particularly sweet to me. She didn't stick any tubes in me and she didn't take any out, either. She came to see me in my room.

"Are you getting along okay?" she inquired.

Whine.

"Bless your heart," she said, adjusting the pillows under my head.

"Would you like for me to rub your face with a wet towel?" she asked.

"If you wouldn't mind," I said, meekly.

When I asked her if she would run down to the convenience store and pick up a couple of six-packs, she refused, however. Whining does have its limits.

Actually, I think I did my best whining at night. They may have lousy lunches at Emory Hospital in Atlanta, but they make terrific milkshakes. I would order a milkshake and then whine my way into a pain pill. After a couple hours sleep, I would awaken and roll over on my back and press the button to call the night nurse.

I never did see her face and I never got her name, but the night nurse was an angel, too.

"You need something?" she would ask me.

I'd whine yes.

"Water?"

I'd whine no.

"Back rub?"

I'd whine yes.

"That feel good?"

I'd whine another yes.

"Had enough?"

I'd whine another no.

The perfect woman, I decided, would own a beer joint and rub your back for as long as you wanted her to.

They made me get up out of bed and walk once I was back in my room. I would walk up the hall and then back down it again. It got easier each time I tried it, although it was weeks before I could actually walk completely upright. Stooped over like that got me more sympathy, however.

They also made me wear white stockings, which were very tight and which were supposed to improve the circulation in my legs. They looked like what baseball players call sanitary hose. Every morning, the orderly would come into my room and put fresh stockings on me. One morning, he asked if I wanted to try putting on my own stockings. I whined my way out of that and even convinced him to go get me a newspaper.

I turned to the sports section first. North Carolina was even closer to the national basketball championship, and the Cubs still couldn't beat a team make up of night nurses.

I received a lot of cards and flowers in the hospital. I also received some gifts. I have a friend who runs a men's clothing store. He sent me a shirt. It fit. Another friend sent me a caricature of myself ogling a nurse in a tight skirt. That fit, too. The only thing I do better than ogle is whine.

I also got candy and fruit baskets and jars of peanuts and boxes of pecans and a Valvoline T-shirt and cap, and one day they even delivered balloons to my room. Cards and flowers and gifts and balloons are nice. They say people give a damn.

A little girl of nine or ten or so occupied the room directly across from mine. I thought I had trouble. She had two faulty valves. They both had been replaced.

Crowds gathered in my room. We ate the fruit and nuts and we laughed amongst the cards and flowers and balloons.

The little girl was alone. One of the nurses told me about her. She was from a poor family in another state. Her mother hadn't accompanied her for the operation.

"She's frightened nearly to death," said one of the nurses, "but she hasn't whined once."

I got the message.

The nurses helped me out of my bed and I walked over to the little girl's room. Her eyes. That's where most of the fear was, in her eyes.

I asked her questions. She would only nod her answers.

"Do you have any brothers and sisters?" I asked.

She nodded yes.

"How many?"

I think she tried to count them in her head, but poor families run big, and it's tough to keep track of the exact number who are sharing your attempt to survive.

"Maybe now that you are well," I said, "you can run around and play with all your brothers and sisters."

Maybe that thought hadn't crossed her mind as yet. Her nod was a bit more enthusiastic than the others had been.

I went back to my room and got back into my bed. Somebody had tied my balloons so they hovered above my head. I have always like balloons. They remind me of circuses and celebrations.

I called for a nurse and told her to take my balloons over and give them to the little girl. I don't deserve any applause for that. I should have thought of it earlier. Little girls with frightened and lonely eyes and bright, bouncing balloons deserve to be together.

If Love Were Oil, I'd Be About a Quart Low: Lewis Grizzard on Women *wasn't the first choice of a title for Lewis Grizzard's fifth book. In fact, much of the preliminary publicity was done under the title* Cordie Mae Poovey Was a Good Ol' Gal. *(Cordie Mae is a well-known figure for Grizzard aficionados; she tormented many a recess during Grizzard's elementary school days and has been immortalized in several of Grizzard's stories.)* If Love Were Oil, I'd Be About a Quart Low *eventually won out as the title; it captures the feel of the book, but also plays a bit with the reader's knowledge of Grizzard's earlier works. Only those few very careful readers would remember the line from the very end of* They Tore Out My Heart and Stomped That Sucker Flat : *"If somebody hasn't written [a song] called, 'If My Heart Was a Pick-Up Truck, It Would Be a Quart Low,' then they should."*

If love were oil, I'd be about a quart low

Lewis Grizzard

on women

1983

# •Constipation and the Dreaded Copperheaded Water Rattler

"No matter how old a man gets, the surest cure for his ills is to have a woman around to treat him like a little boy, because as soon as a man feels the slightest thing wrong with his health, he immediately reverts to his earliest childhood."

**O**ne of my very first memories involves a tricycle accident that I had when I was perhaps three years old. I pedaled my tricycle off the front porch of our house. I don't recall why I did something so foolish, but I do recall learning from the experience that if I cried as long and as loud as I possibly could, my mother soon would arrive on the scene and ease whatever trauma had befallen me.

She picked me up, held my aching head, and then gave me ice cream so that I would stop crying. Whenever I wanted ice cream after that, I would pedal my tricycle off our front porch. My mother eventually caught on to that trick; had she not, I might have wound up with severe brain damage, all in the name of two large scoops of chocolate ice cream.

Women do have a way of caring for a man when he is injured or ill. When I had a stomachache, my mother brought me ginger ale. Ginger ale will do wonders for an aching stomach, especially if it has been poured over ice your mother has placed inside a towel and beaten with a hammer in order to crush it. When I had a cold, she brought me chicken noodle soup and promised that if I ate it all, I could have Fig Newtons for dessert. It's amazing how much chicken noodle soup a small boy can stand, if there is the promise of Fig Newtons afterwards.

No matter how old a man gets, the surest cure for his ills is to have a woman around to treat him like a little boy, because as soon as a man feels the slightest thing wrong with his health, he immediately reverts to his earliest childhood.

"I feel terrible," he whines.

"Where does my little precious hurt?"

"It's my head."

"It's his precious little head."

"It hurts bad."

"I know it does. Let Mommy kiss it and make it all better."

And it always does feel better when a woman kisses it.

The only time a man should *not* tell a woman he isn't feeling well is when he has the slightest hint that he might be constipated.

When I was a child, my mother constantly interrogated me

regarding the state of my bowels. Regardless of what my symptoms might be, she first suspicioned they were the direct result of constipation. If my stomach hurt, she was certain I was constipated. If my head ached, constipation was the cause of it. If I became irritable, what I needed was a good bowel movement.

My mother spent hundreds, perhaps even thousands, of dollars on laxatives during my formative years. At first, she tried to trick me into taking them by offering me chocolate-flavored laxatives. I soon caught on to that ploy, however. I still don't eat anything that is chocolate-flavored if I am going to have to leave my house at any point in the ensuing eighteen hours.

What else my mother did, when she thought I was constipated, was tell the entire world about it. I was with her on a grocery shopping trip once.

"You certainly are a cute little boy," the man weighing vegetables said to me.

"He'll look better when he gets some of his color back," my mother, picking at the tomatoes, replied. "He's been constipated, you know."

"I didn't know," said the man weighing vegetables.

"Oh, yes," my mother continued. "First he started to get irritable, and then..."

I tried to hide my head under the butter bean and eggplant bins. Not only had my mother embarrassed me beyond belief by telling the man I had been constipated, she further insisted on giving him every detail involving my stoppage.

The same thing happened to me when I started school. I was out a couple of days and my mother sent the first grade teacher a note that read, "Please excuse Lewis. He's been terribly constipated, and so I went and bought a box of supposi..."

Every little boy in America can grow up to be president, they taught me in school. But I didn't want to be president. They would interview my mother and she would tell the entire Washington press corps that the reason I had asked Congress for a tax hike was because I was constipated at the time.

I suppose, however, it is the sworn duty of nearly every mother to look after her children, even their bowel habits. In fact, were it not for my mother's hovering attention, I might have died a small boy, from a snakebite, of all things.

We remained in Fort Benning a couple of years after I was born, and then my father received orders to report to Camp Chaffee, Arkansas. That's where the great tricycle crashes took place. That is also where I came into contact with my first—and almost last—snake.

We had a small garage near our house. My mother kept her wringer washing machine there. One morning, while she folded her clothes, I played in the dirt that was the garage floor.

My mother heard a strange, buzzing sound, looked up, and in her horror saw a large rattlesnake only a few feet away from me. It was coiled to strike. Not being aware of the dangers of snakes at my tender age, I showed no apparent intention of trying to remove myself from my perilous position.

As a matter of fact, all I did was sit there like an idiot, eating dirt. My mother screamed out and, in one quick motion, moved toward me and picked me up and whisked me away from the garage and the snake. A road gang was working nearby. One of the guards came and shot the snake.

As much as I was indebted to my mother for saving my life for the first time—there would be other opportunities for her to do the same thing—the snake incident had profound effects on my childhood. One, my mother didn't allow me out of the house alone for several years afterwards. Two, when she did allow me out of her sight, she usually did so with a long warning about looking for snakes. And three, all that combined to make me deathly afraid of any member of the reptile family, especially snakes, but also including lizards and turtles.

When I was older, I went on my first camping trip.

"Make certain," said my mother, "that you check your tent and sleeping bag for snakes."

I did just that. Every hour on the hour, I turned my sleeping bag inside out to make certain no snakes had crawled inside, and then I beat the sides of the tent with a large stick to frighten any other snakes.

"What are you doing?" asked the adult who was supervising the camping trip.

"Running all the snakes out of my tent," I said.

"There aren't any snakes in your tent," he insisted.

"I know," I said. "I just ran them all out."

I have kept this fear of snakes all my life. I stay out of tall weeds, murky water, and the reptile house at the zoo. I don't believe there are snakes that won't bite you, and I don't believe the old axiom that snakes won't bite underwater. Of course, snakes will bite underwater, especially the dreaded copperheaded water rattler, which is so mean that if you check into a Holiday Inn, it will check into the room next to you and then bite you when you go in the pool.

Despite the fact there is a chance you will become paranoid about such things as snakes, having a mother to look after you offers a certain amount of comfort that a man misses when he leaves his mother's nest. I can't imagine growing up without a mother to nurse my ills and save me from tricycle accidents and snakes. Yet I was almost confronted with that very situation.

My mother contracted some sort of rare condition while we lived in Arkansas. It began with an itching scalp. Then her scalp became infected, and they put her in an Army airplane and flew her to Walter Reed Hospital in Washington, D.C. My father and I followed by train.

My mother lost all of her hair. The infection got worse. The doctors thought she was going to die. I can recall visiting her in the hospital. She had bandages all over her head. My father tried to explain the situation. I didn't understand him.

"Your mother is going to go away, son," he said.

"To where, Daddy?" I asked.

"To heaven," he said.

"Why can't we go?"

"We can later."

Heaven. Where was this heaven? What was this heaven? Why couldn't I go there with her? Who was going to hold me when I needed holding? Who was going to give me ice cream when I cried?

My mother didn't die. She didn't have any hair for a long time, but she didn't die. And when her hair grew back months later, it was very special to me, and I would sit in her lap for hours, or lie beside her while she slept, and twirl it back and forth between my fingers.

My mother was even more dedicated to my well-being after her close bout with death. She had had a dream, or at least she thought it was a dream, during her most desperate hours in the hospital. She would tell me the story later:

"In the dream," she began, "I was standing by a beautiful lake, and you were playing in the flowers and shrubs around it. I heard a voice from the other side of the lake. I looked and I saw someone talking to me. The voice was telling me, 'Go back. Don't cross the lake. Your little boy needs you.'"

The voice, she said, was Miss Genie's, my father's mother, my paternal grandmother, who had died eleven months before I was born. They called it a miracle that my mother had lived.

My father was reassigned to Fort Myer, Virginia, just outside of Washington in Arlington, during my mother's hospital stay. We remained there after she was released. Those were priceless days, filled with long walks at my mother's side. Often, we would walk amongst the graves in Arlington National Cemetery, and she would tell me of war and of the soldiering heroics of my father. There was wonderful time spent with him, too, and he taught me all sorts of marvelous things, including how to say the word "bullshit." My father thought the fact that his young son could say "bullshit" was hilarious, and he would take me around to his buddies on the post, and I would get to say "bullshit" ten or fifteen times before the visit was over.

One thing he did not tell me, however, was that there was a time to say "bullshit" and a time *not* to say "bullshit." One isn't born with that kind of knowledge. However, I soon did learn that one of the times it is absolutely mandatory not to say "bullshit" is when the chaplain has come to your house for a visit.

"Hi there, young man." said the chaplain as he entered our living room.

"Bullshit," said I.

After they had revived my mother and the chaplain had left, she instructed my father to take me into my bedroom and to quote her, "teach this child never to say words like that again," which even I understood really meant, "beat this child senseless."

My father obviously felt a party to my indiscretion, so he devised a plan. He would strike the closet door with his belt, and I would scream out in pain with each lick.

"Wham!" went the belt against the door.

"Waaaaaa!" I cried out.

Three or four "whams" and "waaaas" later we both got tickled and began to laugh. My mother opened the door. She tried to get the belt away from my father so she could render the punishment herself—to both of us. My parents wrestled playfully, and then they fell on my bed and I jumped in between them, and we all laughed our-selves silly. I think, in retrospect, that at the moment, I felt as much love as I have ever felt. On future occasions of spiritual revelry, it re-mained a comfort to think that perhaps some knowing, seeing, power knew of the scarcity of our time left together and saw to it that we had such moments. If that is, indeed, the case, then blessed be He who provided them.

They remain my treasure.

My mother tried to explain Korea to me and why my father had to go there.

"Is that near heaven, Mama?"

"No, son. Far from it," she said.

I didn't understand her explanation, of course, just as I had not understood when my father tried to explain why my mother was go-ing away.

All I knew was that one day my father took me into his arms and squeezed me, and he told me to take care of my mother, and then he stepped on another train, and he was gone. We were back on a train ourselves, my mother and I, in a few weeks. We took the Seaboard Silver Comet south. We would wait out the war with my grandpar-ents, C. B. and Willie Word.

After their children all left Heard County and their health began to fail, C. B. and Willie also abandoned the family place and moved near their oldest daughter, Jessie, thirty miles away in Coweta County. They settled in a sleepy hamlet named Moreland, population three hun-dred, and likely that many dogs and twice as many chickens. C. B. bought twelve acres that sat behind the Baptist Church's cemetery and built himself a home there, and he busied himself keeping his acres in corn and potatoes, both sweet and Irish, and plum trees and scuppernong vines.

I missed my father during those days, but I was drawn even closer to my mother. My spoiling was well under way. My grandfather, "Daddy Bun" to me, was the kind of man who attracted dogs and small chil-dren, so I spent a lot of time with him. He had little education, but he was a man of many talents, not the least of which were tossing a baseball to his four-year-old grandson, cutting off chickens' heads (the rest of which would be Sunday dinner), building homemade kites, catching fish, and shooting rabbits and squirrels.

We had a group prayer each night before we went to bed. Daddy Bun, Mama Willie, my mother, and I would gather in the tiny living room, drawing close to the kerosene stove that warmed the house. My grandfather would give thanks for rain, and then he would ask for the blessing of peace that would bring the boys back from Korea.

One night, my grandfather asked me to pray.

"What should I pray about, Daddy Bun?" I asked him.

"Pray your daddy is safe," he said.

I did.

The next day, I was with Daddy Bun in his fields. I asked him if God really heard prayers.

"He does," he said.

"Think my daddy's safe?" I asked.

"No way to know for certain, son," he said. "All we can do is keep praying."

My father was missing in action, the telegram said. His outfit had been surprised, and although his body had not been found, he was presumed dead with the rest of his comrades.

My mother drew me ever closer to her in those awful days after the telegram. I suppose any woman who thinks she has lost her man sees their child as a part of the husband, as a product of their love, and clings to that child for some sense of relief. I spent both days and nights at my mother's side. Often I would awaken to her sobbing into a pillow. At those times, I would hold her hand and twirl her hair between my fingers.

One miracle had saved my mother. I needed another to save my father. I got it. A second telegram arrived some weeks later, saying that he had been found, that he was alive, and that he would be coming home. My father called from Pearl Harbor on a Christmas Eve, and my mother cried again that night, too, but there is such a thing as sobbing happily, and I could tell the difference.

We were always getting on and off of trains in the early days of my life. Another one pulled into Atlanta's Union Station one afternoon, and my father stepped off. He was much thinner than I remembered him. We all hugged and we all cried some more, and then we sat and ate from a shoe box filled with fried chicken that Mama Willie had brought along.

We went back to Fort Benning after that. He was a captain by then, and the Army had given him a soft job as the base athletic director. I would sit on his lap as he coached the basketball team, and it seemed like he had never gone away, and he told me he would never go away again.

"They've taken all the fight this soldier has," I remember his saying to my mother.

We built a house in Columbus, and I started school. There were more ball games, and we went to movies together, the three of us; and one summer my father packed up my mother and me and Daddy Bun and Mama Willie, and we all went to Florida in our 1950 Hudson my father called the "Blue Goose." My father bought Daddy Bun some beer one night, and my grandfather drank a couple down and got a little high and began to hum, "What a Friend We Have in Jesus." I never knew why.

My grandmother did not hold to drinking, however, not even a couple of beers on a Florida vacation. There is nothing so loud or fearsome, I would learn later, as a woman raging against the evils of alcohol, especially if her foursquare opposition to drink is built on a Biblical foundation. Mama Willie gave my grandfather one of the fiercest tongue-lashings my tender ears had ever heard, ending with the Biblical allusion, "A drunkard shall not enter the Kingdom of Heaven!" Daddy Bun just kept humming.

I first noticed something was wrong between my parents when they stopped sleeping in the same bed. My father moved into a third bedroom, and I would go first to his bed at night and he would tell me stories, and I would rub the back of his head and feel the shrapnel still lodged there. Then I would go into my mother's room and, often, I would catch her crying again. Sometimes, I would go to sleep beside her, still twirling her hair between my fingers.

Then there were arguments, most centered around my father's drinking, and he would be gone for days. When he came back, he would be unshaven and he would reek of a smell that was foreign to me. Then men in uniform began coming to our house to look for him, and my mother would tell them he was ill.

He said strange things in those days. He talked about men he had seen die around him, and he would awaken us with screams in the night, and some nights he wouldn't even go to bed. He would sit at our kitchen table and pour an amber liquid out of a bottle into a glass, and then he would talk on the telephone for what seemed like hours, and he would be sobbing into it.

The day it ended, I was sitting in my desk in the first-grade room at Rosemont Elementary School in Columbus. It was springtime. Six weeks were left in my first school year. The door to my room had a window in it. That day, that last day, I looked up into the window in the door and I saw the Army insignia on my father's hat. He walked into my room in the middle of class, whispered something to my teacher, and then motioned for me to come with him.

When we were in the car, he told me that my mother had gone to visit Daddy Bun and Mama Willie for a few days, and that he and I were going on a trip.

He had a bag packed for me. We drove to Atlanta and we boarded another train. We stopped in some strange place called Columbia, South Carolina, and stayed in a motel for several days. My father, I noticed, was no longer wearing his uniform.

After that, we caught another train, and we visited relatives I had never seen before in another town I had never seen before, Savannah. I hadn't talked to my mother in more than a week.

"Is Mama coming to see us?" I would ask.

"Soon," said my father.

Another week, and then we were on a third train, this time to Portsmouth, Virginia, where there were more relatives. My father never went outside the house very much in Portsmouth, and when he did go out, it was only at night. I still hadn't heard from my mother. I missed her.

My father had gone AWOL, I discovered later. Thirteen years of service were going down the drain. The man had been through two wars. He had Purple Hearts and a Bronze Star, but the strain of two wars had been too much, and then the drinking had started and the arguments had followed.

So one day when my mother had gone off to work, my father had hit the air and had taken me with him.

My mother was frantic when she got out of the car in front of the house where we were staying in Portsmouth. She had gone to my Uncle Frank, the lawyer, and he had tracked us from Atlanta to Columbia and then to Savannah and then to Virginia, and he had driven my mother to Portsmouth to get me.

What was happening? Why all the loud voices? I was happy to have both parents again, but I didn't have them as I wanted them. They were enemies.

"Mama," I asked, "why are you and daddy fighting?"

"He's sick, son," she answered me. "Your daddy is very sick, and you have to go with me so that he can get well."

We drove all night back to Atlanta in my Uncle Frank's car, and since there was no other option—my mother couldn't hold the house in Columbus on a teacher's pay—we went back to the little house in Moreland, back to live with Daddy Bun and Mama Willie.

They drummed my father out of the Army as unfit to continue, and he set to roaming and drinking more and more. I would see him only occasionally after that, but each time he would promise that some-day soon, he would come tapping on the window outside the room where my mother and I slept, and he would say, "Christine, Christine...I've come to get you and my son," and we would leave and be together again. And I would ask, "For always, Daddy?" and he would answer, "For always."

I listened for his voice night after night, and I lived on the hope that one night I would hear it. But it never came.

Sometimes at night, when I didn't do it on my own, my mother would ask me to hold her hand and twirl her hair between my fingers.

# • Happiness is a Red-Headed Cheerleader

"The first cheerleader to catch my eye during my freshman year of high school was a dazzling fourteen-year-old redhead from a well-to-do Newnan family. She whirled with the best of them, and she did seem to show some spark of interest when I hit her with my classic opening line, 'Do you think professional wrestling is fake?' "

**B**un Word died in the spring of my first year in high school. He was seventy-three, yet he was still working his fields just as hard as before. Even after my mother and stepfather and I moved into our new house, I spent many evenings with him. My grandparents had a television by then, and he and I watched it together.

He enjoyed baseball games, wrestling matches, westerns, and Billy Graham specials. He hated "The Ed Sullivan Show," because most weeks about all Ed had to offer was a magician or two, some trained seals, and an opera singer. We were watching the program one Sunday evening anyway, and Ed Sullivan introduced Anna Maria Alberghetti, who shook the windows with her voice. Daddy Bun watched and listened for a few moments, and then replied, "If that woman can sing, my ass is a typewriter." As he walked out of the room, he said to me, "Call me when the seals come out."

The old mule had died by then, and Daddy Bun was following his little Briggs and Stratton garden tractor up a row one April afternoon when he felt the first pains in his chest. He was never one to complain. But the pains became so intense that he struggled back to his house and sat down in a chair, hoping the crushing feeling would go away. My grandmother knew there was something wrong by the fact that he had come inside, apparently to rest. Nothing could bring him in from the fields, short of gully-washing rain.

"Are you all right, Daddy?" she asked him.

He did not reply, however. He hurt too much to speak.

My grandmother rushed to our house, and my mother and I went to him and somehow managed to get him inside our car. We drove him to the only hospital in the county, six miles away in Newnan. He revived a bit on the way, and by the time he was rolled into the emergency room, he had already started to apologize to everyone for causing a disturbance.

A day later, he had improved to the point he was begging to go home from the hospital and get back to his fields. The doctors dismissed him the day after he had been admitted. They did advise him, however, to slow down a bit, but he didn't listen. His family had been advising him to ease off on his work for years, but without his garden and his tractor, he likely wouldn't have lived as long as he did.

Four days after he came home from the hospital, I had supper with my grandparents. Mama Willie made her square-ended cornbread and fried a hen. Daddy Bun seemed in uncommonly good spirits that night. After eating we played a couple of hands of Rook, and then I left to attend revival services at the Baptist church a few yards from my grandparents house.

The visiting preacher was just about to call for the invitational hymn, "Just As I Am," when one of my cousins came into the church and whispered something to my mother, who was sitting next to me.

She jumped out of her seat and ran toward the door. I suppose I knew what was happening, even without being been told, but I didn't want to believe it.

When I reached my grandparents' house, H. B. was bent over Daddy Bun, who was lying in his bed. My mother and my Aunt Jessie were crying, and Mama Willie's face was frozen with fear.

Daddy Bun's eyes were closed, and his face was turning blue. H. B., a large man with powerful arms, was pushing on his chest, attempting to start his heart beating. The ambulance arrived and they put Daddy Bun on the stretcher. I held the front door open as they rolled him down the steps. My grandfather's mouth was open and there was no sign of life to him.

Somebody said later that he probably died in his bed. Mama Willie said she thought he did, too, and she would give this account of the final moments she shared with her husband of more than fifty years:

"I had just turned off the light," she began, "and Daddy was on his side of the bed, and I was on mine. All of a sudden, he rolled over and put his arm around me, and he kissed me and he tried to say something, but I felt him go limp. And when I tried to get him to answer me, he didn't say anything."

One last kiss and then he died. Even at fourteen, I was charmed and warmed by that, and there was something else that pleased me, too. I remember that my grandmother never went to bed with snuff in her mouth.

The funeral took all day. First, we drove back to his home church, Pleasant Grove Baptist in Heard County, and three preachers I had never seen before took turns at the pulpit. It was just the kind of service my grandfather would have wanted.

None of the three preachers had any prepared notes, I was positive, because nobody could have read that fast. They would start out slowly, but by the time each had reached the climax of his message, his coat would be off, his tie would be undone, his shirt would be wringing wet with perspiration, and he would be gasping for breath every five or six sentences that would come rushing out of his mouth in powerful gusts. It was impossible to keep up with what the preachers were trying to say, but I was able to pick up a "Pah-raise his name!" here and a "Have you been washed in the buh-lud?" there, and so I at least knew the general subject matter.

There were a couple of things I would have changed about my grandfather's funeral, however. It was the custom then to bring the body back home after the undertaker had completed his work, and friends and family would then gather, and one by one they would stand over the casket and peer in at the departed. The closest family members usually broke down when they looked at the body of their loved one, but friends usually didn't cry. They simply stared awhile and then remarked, "Lord, Lord, he looks like he could just sit up and talk, don't he?"

Actually, my grandfather didn't look like he could just sit up and talk at all, and even if he had, his first words likely would have been an apology for the way he was dressed. They put him in a banker's suit and put a white shirt and tie on him, and they took off his glasses. And if I hadn't been with him practically every day of my life since I was seven, I might not have recognized him.

They should have dressed him in one of his old shirts and in his work pants, and they shouldn't have put all that powdery gook on his face. And had it been left up to me, I would have put the *Market Bulletin* in the casket with him, so that when he got to heaven, he could have looked in the classifieds at what they were getting for mules around the state, one of his favorite pastimes.

After the services in Heard County, we brought him all the way back to Moreland to bury him in the family plot. Unfortunately, there had been no more room available in the Baptist cemetery near his house when Daddy Bun and Mama Willie decided it was time to plan for where they would go to rest. So they had reluctantly bought in the Methodist cemetery a mile or so away from their house.

There was one other thing I would have changed. It was, indeed, fitting that they had a girl from the community sing "What a Friend We Have in Jesus" when we got to his graveside, but I would have asked her to hum the last two verses.

Mama Willie refused to move out of their little house after Daddy Bun died. I didn't blame her very much, and I even agreed to spend the night with her in my old bedroom. She wasn't in the best of health, either, and the family was afraid to leave her alone nights.

My grandmother changed a lot after Daddy Bun died. She wasn't nearly as spirited. Her memory began to go. I could hear her talking to "Daddy" in her sleep, and sometimes, when I sat with her at night, her conversation would wander, and she would discuss occurrences of long ago as if I were Daddy Bun. I never tried to correct her, and I actually enjoyed sharing with her some of the things she had shared with him. I also made certain that at least once a week, when I came down to her house to spend the night, I brought a little can of Brutton's with me.

"You always were a sweet boy," she would say to me. I sort of wished she would send me for one more switch, just for old times' sake.

After the children from the little community of Moreland finished the eighth grade, they were then picked up in county buses in front of the old schoolhouse each morning and transported to Newnan High School, a huge educational plant that was quite unsettling to those of us from the hinterlands.

We also were confronted with some difficulty in being totally accepted by our classmates who had grown up in Newnan, one of the wealthiest towns per capita in the country. None of the Moreland boys had the word that white socks were out, for instance, and we first laughed at the colorful footwear the Newnan boys sported before we found out they were the very latest style at a dollar-fifty a pair.

We also learned that the correct shoe to wear was made by Bass and was called a "Weejun," that Madras shirts were a must and they should have a button in the back of the collar, that pants needed to be pegged at the cuff so that the colored socks would show, and that if you didn't have a beige London Fog raincoat to wear, you were a total country hick whose social opportunities were limited to showing a hog or a cow at the Future Farmers of America-sponsored agriculture show at the annual county fair.

I had no intentions of being ostracized thusly, so I went to my mother after my third day of high school and asked her for money to purchase myself a new wardrobe. When she heard that colored socks cost a dollar-fifty a pair, and that I had to have shirts that were imported from India, along with other expensive accessories, she nearly fainted. She was still bringing home the meager salary of a county elementary schoolteacher, and my stepfather had fallen on hard times trying to sell a-dollar-and-a-deed-is-all-you-need shell homes.

She wouldn't go more than two pairs of socks, one Madras shirt, and a couple of new pairs of pants, but she did allow me at least that. I helped my Uncle Hugh Dorsey pull his corn one entire weekend for half what the Weejuns cost, and I got the rest by selling "Pig" Landers my lunchroom dessert every day for a month. Pig had an appetite that was legend. One day when we were still in grammar school in Moreland, some of the men who used to play checkers in front of Cureton and Cole's store asked Pig if he thought he could eat a particularly large watermelon that was for sale in the store.

"We'll buy it if you can eat it," they said to Pig, who surprised us by asking if he could go home first. He returned a few minutes later and said he thought he could, indeed, eat a watermelon that size, and he proceeded to do just that, gnawing well into the rind before he was finished.

"That's some kinda eatin', boy," said one of the men. "But why'd you have to go home first?"

"We had one in the icebox about the same size," said Pig. "I went home and ate that one just to make sure I could eat this one."

Thanks to the generosity of my mother, my corn-pulling efforts, and Pig Landers' appetite, I managed to dress myself in a fashion consistent with that of my more affluent classmates, and afterwards I turned my attention to one of my new school's most exciting benefits.

My eighth grade class in Moreland had totalled less than thirty, and only about half of those were girls, and five or six of them you wouldn't take to a rat-killing. But high school! There were girls everywhere, and more bosoms than I had ever seen under one roof.

(Be ever mindful, however, that I had yet to see but one pair of unclothed breasts, those of the talented Boom-Boom LaTouche. Another chance had gone by the boards later when a group of my friends and I learned through the grapevine that Sherleen Gimple—whose daddy, Farnon, ran a brisk chenille bedspread and memorial marker business out front of his house—always took a tub bath about eight o'clock in the evening, and that if you were quiet about it, it was very possible to climb up in a tree outside the Gimple's bathroom window and get the show of your life. Trembling with the same anticipation that had been ours when we saw Boom-Boom at the fair—and feeling smug in the fact there would be no admission charge—we sneaked up the tree shortly before eight one evening and waited for Sherleen, who had a set known for miles around, to take her bath.

When the light went on, we could barely keep from welcoming Sherleen with a rousing cheer, but imagine our disappointment when the figure we saw through the window was fat old Farnon Gimple taking off his overalls. The one night we chose to try to get a glimpse of Sherleen, her daddy decided to take his weekly bath.)

Despite the fact the female population at Newnan High was larger than what I was used to by a hundredfold, I was still being hampered in replacing the long-gone Shirley Ann by two factors:

One, I had just turned fourteen and was still two long, agonizing years away from having my driver's license. Whereas Willard Haines and only a few other older boys in Moreland had cars, high school was filled with licensees from the eleventh and twelfth grades, and they were constantly shopping in the lower grades for dates, because girls their age were dating college boys by that time. Obtaining female companionship in the formative years is an eat-the-next-fish-smaller-than-you sort of proposition.

Two, and this is something I hadn't counted on, there was a sort of loose, unwritten rule that implored county riffraff to keep away from the well-coiffed, well-dressed young ladies of the city establishment. That problem could be overcome, I noticed, if one happened to be an athlete or was willing to settle for one of the uglier Newnan girls, who were just as desperate for attention as the county fellows.

I decided to try the athletic route. Because I had taken my physical appearance from my mother's side of the family—I was quite thin—I decided not to risk my life playing football, as much as I figured that was the sport with the most potential for latching on to a Newnan girl. Instead, I went out for the junior varsity basketball team. I made the squad and became an immediate starter.

I thought perhaps my first move would be on a member of the

girls' junior varsity team; but it was at that point I learned something else about females of that era—if they played basketball, it meant they hadn't made it as a cheerleader and didn't mind working up a sweat in public, both of which made me suspect of their potential, as far as future romantic possibilities were concerned.

I also stayed as far away as possible from the girls' basketball team in high school, because good ol' Alice McTavish from Virginia Reel days was a member, and she had grown even bigger and stronger. I remained constantly afraid that she would rekindle her affection for me, and I didn't think my frail physique could take it, especially now that the Twist was the popular dance of the time. She might have caught me broadside with one of her hips, and I could see myself rolling across the dance floor as Chubby Checker sang away.

The way they played girls' basketball in those days was three girls, the forwards, shot at the basket while three others, the guards, played defense on the other end. It didn't really matter how they played when Alice McTavish was in the game, however.

One of the problems most women have in sports is their basic inability to jump very high. There wasn't a girl in the state who could get above Alice McTavish's outreached, blacksmith-like arms. The Newnan offense was simply for Alice to stand under the basket. When the ball was passed to her, she turned and shot it at the hoop.

It would seem that Newnan would have been a powerhouse in girls' basketball, with Godzilla underneath the basket, but Alice was as clumsy and as uncoordinated as she was ugly and large. Often she would shoot the ball over and over again, getting her own rebound each time, only to have time to run out in the quarter before she could get the ball into the basket. Newnan lost a great many 8–6 games in girls' basketball during the McTavish era.

Alice was rarely called on to dribble. However, in a close game one night, she received a pass from the guards over the center line, and turned only to find herself still several feet out of what may be loosely referred to as her shooting range.

It never occurred to her to pass the ball to one of her teammates, and the sight of Alice trying to dribble the ball toward the basket had everyone in the gym howling with laughter. After a couple of bounces, the ball went sailing off one of Alice's size-fourteen high-tops and out of bounds. Alice put her hands on her hips and, in a voice that could best be described as a bellow, uttered an unprintable oath loud enough for the entire audience and the people in line at the concession stand to hear it.

The referee standing closest to her had no choice but to attempt to eject her from the game. Alice refused to sit down, however, and when the official insisted, she let him have one in the belly. Alice continued to play the remainder of the game. They called one of the shop teachers to come out of the stands to take the injured referee's place, while he was trying to catch his breath.

Having thus decided to avoid girl basketball players, I turned my attention to the cheerleaders. Making cheerleader at Newnan High School was a great and highly sought-after honor. The students elected the cheerleading team after a series of tryouts, in which each entrant was asked to perform a series of cheers and acrobatics in front of the entire student body. Girls were supposed to be chosen on the basis of originality of cheer, tumbling ability, range of voice, and whether or not they would be outstanding representatives of their school, community, and parents during interscholastic events. I always voted on the basis of which girl showed the most of her underpants when she whirled around in her cheerleading skirt.

The first cheerleader to catch my eye during my freshman year of high school was a dazzling fourteen-year-old redhead from a well-to-do Newnan family. She whirled with the best of them , and she did seem to show some spark of interest when I hit her with my classic opening line, "Do you think professional wrestling is fake?"

As a matter of fact, I fell quite hard and fast for this young beauty, and I thought I had scored further points with her when I allowed her to look on my paper during an ancient history exam, which tested our knowledge of the Punic Wars. She had no idea Rome and Carthage were even mad at each other, much less that they had actually squared off on the fields of combat.

I was soon to learn, however, that this new object of my affection didn't care if I was a brilliant conversationalist and more than willing to share my knowledge of ancient history with her. She already had a boyfriend, and he was an eleventh grader, with a car, who played football. I thought of trying the old popsicle trick on her, and my dog wouldn't have anything to do with me as it was, so that difference would one more name change make?

However, I finally accepted the fact these tactics were no longer workable on any girl over twelve. I simply had no way to fight back against the overwhelming odds that faced me. I looked ahead, and all I could see were two more years of being just another skinny basketball player from the sticks, whose mother still had to drive him around. I thought of petitioning the state legislature to lower the driving age in order to save me from this companionless state, but in my most desperate hour, I got lucky. It all started with a hayride.

**E**lvis Is Dead and I Don't Feel So Good Myself *is the nostalgic account of Lewis Grizzard's attempt to survive in a changing world. Sex, music, clothes, commercials—everything receives the Grizzard treatment.* Elvis is Dead *compares the simplicity of the fifties and early sixties with the ever-changing eighties. His comments about the differences in the eras reveal a great deal about his own sense of himself: "Although I live in a new world, I was reared to live in the old one." While Grizzard may not feel so good in the face of this new world, his social commentary and humor make his readers feel just fine. In fact,* Elvis is Dead *was Grizzard's first book to make it all the way to the* New York Times *Best Seller List.*

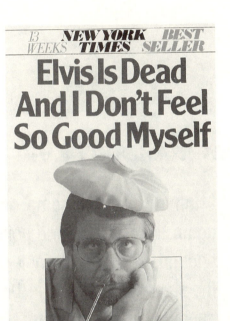

1 9 8 4

# •Camelot in Bloody Ruin

"Nothing was the same after that. Ever again. I trace my world going completely bananas back to that single moment when the shots first cracked in Dallas. What, if anything, has made sense since?"

"Let the word go forth from this time and place...that the torch has been passed to a new generation of Americans..."

—*John F. Kennedy, January 20, 1961*

There was one family of Catholics in Moreland in 1960. They had to drive ten miles to the county seat to go to church. I didn't think there was anything particularly different about them except that on Fridays, when the rest of us were attempting to force down what they said was meatloaf but tasted like Alpo looks, the kids from the Catholic family were eating what appeared to be a tasty serving of fried fish. Had it not been for the fact that it would have put the good Methodists and Baptists in my family into shock and running fits, I might have become a Catholic, too, just to avoid the Friday meatloaf.

The adults in town didn't trust Catholics. One of the old men down at the store said he heard they stole babies. Somebody else said Catholics drank a lot, and half the time they didn't even speak English when they were holding church services.

John Kennedy frightened the local voting bloc, perhaps a hundred-or-so strong. He was a Catholic and his daddy was rich, and despite the fact we're talking lifelong Democrats here, they were having a difficult time accepting the idea that a person with religious beliefs so foreign to their own might actually occupy the White House.

The old men around the stove:

"I ain't sure we ought to elect no Cathlic."

"I ain't votin' for him. He'd take all his orders from the Vaddican."

"The what?"

"The Vaddican."

"Where's that?"

"Itly."

"Reckon that's so?"

"Course it's so. Them Cathlics stick together like buttermilk sticks to your chin."

"You ever know'd any Cathlics?"

"Naw, but I think one come in the truckstop a week or so ago."

"How'd you know it was a Cathlic?"

"He's wearing a white shirt. Who else 'round here wears white shirts?"

If Elvis was the first break between the Baby Boomers and their parents, then John Kennedy—at least in rural Georgia, which was my only horizon at the time—was a second. Kennedy never started the youthful explosion that Elvis had, but there was something about the man that appealed to us. It was later described as "vigah." Although I was too young to vote in the 1960 presidential election, I did my part to elect Kennedy by running down Richard Nixon.

I was born under Truman and then came Ike. The General was okay, but I didn't like the way Nixon, his vice president for eight years, looked even then. He already had those jowls, and when he talked, it seemed like his mouth was full of spit and he needed to swallow.

I also was never able to understand how Nixon fathered any children, because I was convinced he slept in his suit. I suspect Richard Nixon was born wearing a tiny little suit and tie, and his aunts and uncles probably stood around his crib and looked at his beady little eyes and at his jowls—I'm sure he was born with them, too—and said things like, "Well, let's hope and pray he grows out of it."

He didn't, of course. The older he got, the shiftier he looked, and that's why Kennedy beat him in 1960. When they debated, Nixon looked like a 1952 Ford with a busted tailpipe and foam rubber dice hanging off his rearview mirror; Kennedy was a Rolls Royce in comparison.

All the girls at school liked Kennedy, too. "He's sooo cute," was their usual adept analysis of his platform.

Historians who have looked back on the brief thousand days that John Kennedy was our president have failed to note that Kennedy did, in fact, accomplish an important feat with his looks. Remember his hair? John Kennedy's hair was sort of fluffy. Nixon probably greased his down with whatever it was I used to slick down my ducktails.

In the early 1960s, most men were still using Vitalis and Wildroot Creme Oil on their hair. But I don't think John Kennedy used anything like that on his. In fact, Kennedy may have been the first American male to show off "The Dry Look." It was only a few years after Kennedy became president that we celebrated the death of "The Wethead," and American men poured their hair tonic down the drain and spent millions on blow-dryers and hairspray.

Looks are important to a president, and Kennedy was the most handsome American president since Andrew Jackson—who wasn't any Tom Selleck, but at least he didn't have one of those cherub-looking faces like John Quincy Adams. And he didn't wear a powdered wig.

Look at the appearances of our presidents over the years. The pictures of George Washington that were in our history books made the father of our country look like somebody's sweet little grandmother. Abraham Lincoln was no day at the beach, either, and Rutherford B. Hayes had that long scraggly beard, and William Taft was fat. FDR was fairly handsome, but he used that long cigarette holder that made him appear a bit stuffy, I thought. Truman wore funny hats and bow ties, and Eisenhower was militarily rigid and grandfatherly.

John Kennedy, however, *was* the torchbearer for the new generation. If the times were Camelot, then he was certainly Arthur. He seemed more of an admired, understanding big brother to us than an awesome patriarch ruling from some distant perch.

The youth of the early sixties knew little of the system, other than what we had learned in Civics class, but here was a man with whom we were able to relate—if not to his substance, then most certainly to his style.

The Cuban Missile Crisis brought us even closer to him. He told the Russians where he wanted them to stick their missiles and in the meantime created several marvelously exciting days at my high school. I didn't pay a great deal of attention to the crisis at first. Basketball practice had started, and that had me too occupied to consider the end of the world as we knew it.

I was in Jacob's Drug Store in Newnan eating a banana split the night the president went on television in October of 1962 and told the nation that we were about this far from having to sink a few Russian ships and maybe start World War III. I hesitated and watched and listened for a few moments, but then I went back to the banana split.

The next day at school, however, our principal, Mr. O. P. Evans, called the student body together and began to prepare us for the nuclear attack he seemed certain would come before the noon lunch bell.

Mr. Evans was a tall, forceful man with a deep, booming voice that was a fearful and commanding thing. He ran the school with a Bible in one hand and a paddle in the other. The school was his passion, and even an imminent nuclear attack would not deter him from making certain that we would be a model of order until the last one of us had been melted into a nuclear ash.

We were told that when (I don't think he ever mentioned an "if" anywhere) the call came to Mr. Evans's office (probably direct from Washington) to inform him that the bombs and missiles were on the way , we would be hastened back to assembly for further instructions. At that point, a decision would be made on whether or not to close school and send us home. In the event we could not safely evacuate, we would remain at school and be given subsequent assignments as to where we would bed down for the night.

That idea caused a great stirring of interest among the boys. Would we get to sleep near the girls? Could we slip around and perhaps catch them in nothing but their underpants? Bring on the bombs and missiles. Mr. Evans quickly dashed our hopes, however, by stating that the boys would be herded to the gymnasium, while the girls would sleep at the other end of the school in the cafeteria and the student activities room, where the Coke and candy machines were also located, damn the luck.

He instructed us to bring canned goods to store in our lockers the following day, presuming there was one, in case the school ran out of food and we had to spend the winter inside the building waiting for the fallout to subside. Students also were to bring blankets and soap, an extra toothbrush, and a change of clothes and underwear. The sacks of clothes and underwear were stored on the stage in the assembly room. Having been shut out of actually getting to see our female classmates down to their skivvies, a group of us went for the next best thing and sneaked into the assembly room during the post-lunch period and went through the sacks trying to match girls with panties and bras.

The possibility of an attack did lose some of its glamour, however, when Mr. Evans further announced that as long as a single teacher survived, classes would continue and gum chewing would remain a capital offense.

The attack never came, of course, but we did find out that Gayle Spangler, who always was going off to Atlanta on weekends and was allegedly keeping company with college boys and going to wild fraternity parties, had a pair of panties with the 1962 Georgia Tech football schedule printed on the crotch.

John Kennedy was hailed as a conqueror after backing down the

Russians and their missiles, but the triumphant mood of the country was short-lived. One moment Camelot was there, and the next it lay in bloody ruin.

It was autumn of my senior year. November, 1963. I was changing morning classes. I had just finished Spanish, which I hated. I particularly hated those silly records they played to us in Spanish class.

*"El burro es un animal de Mexico, Espana, y Norte Americana, tambien. Repeata, por favor."*

Thirty students with heavy Southern accents would repeat: "El boorow ez uhn anymahl de Mexeecoh, Espainya, why Gnawertee Amuricainya, tambiann."

I was strolling down the hallway toward geometry class. Something was happening. The teachers had come out into the hall and were herding students into classrooms.

"Don't go to your next class. Come into my room. Quickly," said a teacher to me.

The halls were cleared. There was an eerie silence. Is the place on fire? Have the Russians decided to attack after all? Has somebody been caught chewing gum? I noticed the teacher sitting in the desk in front of me. She was holding back tears.

The voice. I had heard that powerful voice so many times. But now it seemed to crack and strain.

"Your attention please," said Mr. Evans over the intercom. "We have just received word that President John Kennedy has been shot in Dallas. We have no other word at this time. May we all bow our heads in prayer."

I can't remember Mr. Evans's prayer word-for-word. It's been more than twenty years. But I think I can still manage its essence:

*"Gawd, Our Father. We beseech Thee. A brilliant young leader has been shot. He is a man we love. He is a man we trust. He is our president. Our Father, we beseech Thee now to rest Your gentle hand upon this man and to spare him, O Gawd. Spare him, so that he can continue to lead us, to guide us, to keep us safe from our enemies, to show us how to make our country even greater, to bring justice to all our people, to make*

*for these students, who soon will go out into the world alone,
a safe and shining place to live and work and grow fruitful.
Spare John Kennedy, O Gawd. Spare our beloved president.
Amen."*

We raised our heads. No one spoke. Some of the girls cried.

"Maybe it's not true," somebody finally said.

"It's true," said someone else, "or Mr. Evans wouldn't have stopped classes for it."

We waited. I don't know how long we waited. Maybe it was seconds. Maybe it was minutes. Finally, the voice came back again,

"Students and faculty of Newnan High School," Mr. Evans began, "President John Fitzgerald Kennedy is dead."

The class idiot was Harley Doakes, whose father hated Kennedy because he had wanted to desegregate the schools. When Mr. Evans announced that the president was dead, Harley Doakes cheered. Somebody in the back of the room threw a book at him and called him a stupid son of a bitch.

Nothing was the same after that. Ever again. I trace my world going completely bananas back to that single moment when the shots first cracked in Dallas.

What, if anything, has made sense since? John Kennedy was dead and we were left with Lyndon Johnson, who was low enough to pick up a dog by its ears. He proceeds to get us involved up to *our* ears in Vietnam, and when he finally decides he's had enough, here comes Nixon again. Why wouldn't this man just go away?

I had all sorts of trouble trying to decide who I wanted to be president in 1972. Picking between Richard Nixon and George McGovern was like picking between sores in your mouth or a bad case of hemorrhoids. I wanted Nixon out, but I didn't want McGovern in.

McGovern was the hippie candidate. I had been raised a patriot. I reluctantly voted for Nixon. I admit he did a few things. He opened China, although I'm still not sure what good it did. If you've seen one Chinese urn, you've seen them all; I still don't know how to use chopsticks; and I never did like sweet and sour pork.

It was under Nixon that Vietnam finally came to a merciful end, of course, and there was that marvelous, moving moment when the POWs came home, but it was impossible for me to put heroic garb on Richard Nixon. There always was the nagging feeling each time I saw him or listened to him that he was somehow putting a Bobby Entrekin shuck on me.

Watergate was all I needed. There I had been a decade earlier—a high school senior with a crew cut and even clearer-cut ideals and values. Then the president is shot, and next comes Vietnam, and then Martin Luther King is gunned down, and somebody shoots Robert Kennedy, and another assassin puts George Wallace in a wheelchair for life. And on top of that, we find out the current president is, indeed, a crook (not to mention a liar with a filthy mouth) and he's run out of office practically on a rail.

I no longer had any idea what to believe or whom to trust.

I was nearing thirty, and practically every sacred cow I had known had been butchered in one way or another.

Nothing was the same anymore. I had seen students burning campus buildings and students being gunned down on campuses by National Guardsmen.

I had been divorced once by then and was working on a second. Half the country was smoking dope. Gasoline was four times what it cost before. Men were growing their hair over their ears and wearing double-knit trousers.

And they weren't singing the old songs anymore, either. In fact, it was soon after the death of John Kennedy that the music headed somewhere I didn't want to go.

If Elvis was a break between me and my parents and my roots, then it was The Beatles who forced me back toward them.

# •The Great Double-Knit Dilemma

"After I bought my brown dress shirt with no buttons on the collar, I lost complete control and bought myself a double-knit shirt. It didn't have any buttons on the collar, either, and it featured pictures of exotic-looking birds. To accent this outfit, I also purchased a pair of double-knit trousers. I looked like Marlin Perkins taking the afternoon off from hunting baboons in the wilds of Africa for Mutual of Omaha."

When we're young, we naturally attempt to dress as our peers do, lest we be ostracized and laughed at. My wardrobe in college, for instance, consisted of the traditional khaki pants and button-down Gant shirts, a couple of V-neck sweaters, a London Fog raincoat, and a pair of Weejuns.

I also had a couple of pairs of socks, but I wore them only to funerals, weddings, or when I had to visit the dean. It was considered quite the fashion not to wear socks with Weejuns. I didn't know this when I arrived on campus at the University of Georgia, but soon after pledging a fraternity, one of my brothers in the bonds, Wally Walrus we called him, took me aside and explained the business about the socks.

The way we dressed on Deep South campuses in the sixties was, of course, quite different from the way students dressed at those schools where there was much dissent about all that was traditional. I'm happy the movement did not hit in Georgia until I was out of school; otherwise, I might have had to find a secondhand store to buy myself some blue jeans with patches and an old Army jacket, like the kids were wearing while they were taking over the administration building at Hofstra or some such place as that.

The way we dressed back then, and the way I continued to dress for several years out of school, is now called the "preppie look." This style of dress is yet the target of much derision from those who still don't understand that it does make a difference what sort of animal emblem appears on one's shirt. Some things, I would say to them, are simply the result of good breeding and cannot be explained to anyone who wears Hush Puppies.

I *would* say that, but I won't, because I admit there was a time when I became totally confused about what to wear, and there was a time when I also allowed myself to stray from this tradition as far as my clothing was concerned.

I blame all this on Richard Nixon, too. How could one not go off course a bit with all the disillusionment that came with Watergate? It was about the time they caught Nixon up to his ears in justice obstructing that I went out and did something entirely crazy. I bought a new shirt that didn't have any buttons on the collar.

This particular shirt was a dress shirt, and it was sort of a light brown, as I recall. Men not only had started wearing their hair longer, but they also were wearing colorful dress shirts with no buttons on the collars. Since my peers at that point were mostly a bunch of guys who hung around local taverns and belched a lot, I was without any sort of guidance as to what currently was regarded as proper attire for a young man nearing his thirties.

It was about the same time, unfortunately, that the double-knit polyester craze hit full force. I'm not certain who invented double-knit fabrics, but rumor says it was first manufactured in a clothing plant in Fort Deposit, Alabama. This cannot be verified, however, because some years ago a mysterious fire erupted in the warehouse and twenty-six thousand knit leisure suits were destroyed.

The owner, Delbert Gumbatz, was last seen catching the bus to Montgomery. He was wearing a Big Orange leisure suit—a favorite among Tennessee football fans. The last person to see him was the insurance man who signed the check for the fire, which, incidentally, smoldered for nearly six months.

Most everybody was wearing some sort of polyester or double-knit in those days, especially at bowling alleys and Moose Club dances. Such material was so popular, in fact, that several people were severely injured when they were trampled by a mob of shoppers in Good Sam, Ohio, who had just been informed, "Attention, K-Mart shoppers. On aisle seven tonight we have a special on men's leisure suits—all you can haul out of here for $29.95."

After I bought my brown dress shirt with no buttons on the collar, I lost complete control and bought myself a double-knit shirt. It didn't have any buttons on the collar, either, and it featured pictures of exotic-looking birds. To accent this outfit, I also purchased a pair of double-knit trousers. I looked like Marlin Perkins taking the afternoon off from hunting baboons in the wilds of Africa for Mutual of Omaha.

It could have been worse, of course. I could have bought myself a Nehru jacket and one of those medallions on a chain that people who wore Nehru Jackets wore around their necks. What stopped me was an experience I had with a friend on the way to lunch one day. He was resplendent in his white Nehru jacket, a pair of white pants, and white patent-leather shoes. His medallion had a picture of Art Garfunkel on it. I was thinking how sharp he looked when three kids stopped him on the street and wanted to buy Eskimo Pies from him. Then two teenagers thought he was the leader of some religious cult and offered their week's supply of marijuana and asked him to bless their headbands.

I chilled on the Nehru suit.

Later, I considered buying myself a leisure suit, maybe a baby blue one to wear with my Marlin Perkins jungle shirt. I went as far as going into a men's store and asking to see their selection.

"I would like to see a leisure suit," I said to the clerk, who was chewing gum and wearing enough polyester to start his own bingo parlor.

"And what color did we have in mind?" he asked me between chomps on his Juicy Fruit.

"Blue," I said.

"Navy, midnight, morning sky or baby?"[a] he asked.

"Baby," I said.

He brought out something from the newly-created Tennessee Ernie Ford line, perfect for a night of dining and dancing in the Billy Budd Room at the local Holiday Inn.

"It's you," said the clerk.

"No, it's not," I said. "It's a conventioneer from Nebraska sipping a piña colada and trying to get up the courage to ask a fat girl with a beehive hairdo to dance." I left the store and never considered buying a leisure suit again.

Soon, however, I was once again faced with a dilemma concerning men's fashion: Would I, or would I not buy myself a neck chain?

Neck chains were big in singles bars in those days. I suppose that was because women were changing, too, and they had shamelessly indicated that the sight of men's chest hairs made them tingle in places they used to deny they even had, until their husbands pressed them on their wedding nights. So men quit wearing undershirts and started leaving their shirts unbuttoned to their navels, and I suppose neck chains and medallions were a way for men not to feel their chests were totally naked.

I happened to be blessed with a great deal of chest hair, and I readily imagined myself at singles bars covered with young women who wanted to run their fingers through it. So I put on my jungle shirt, buttoned only the bottom button, and went out amongst the night.

Not a single young woman expressed a desire to run her fingers through my chest hair, but I did scare off a dog in the parking lot when he saw my shirt.

I decided a neck chain was what I was missing, so I went the next day to a jewelry store.

"Do you have chains for men?" I asked the clerk.

"You kinky devil," he said.

"I beg your pardon," I replied.

"Didn't mean to insult you," the clerk went on. "I like a little S and M myself occasionally."

"S and M?" I said, completely puzzled.

"Don't kid with me," the clerk said. "We don't have any chains here, but I know where you can get a great deal on whips and leather underwear."

I decided that perhaps I wasn't ready for neck chains just yet. Luckily, however, a friend of mine had just returned from California and had the answer—a string of beads. At first, I was a bit wary of them.

"What's that around your neck?" I asked him.

"Beads," he said. "Everybody in California is wearing beads."

"Isn't that a little, well, sissy?" I asked.

"Get off my back with your macho trip," said my friend. "This is 1974."

*Macho.* What was this *macho*? Some sort of Mexican dish he had eaten in California? My friend explained.

"What *macho* means," he began, "is a man trying to be like John Wayne all the time—aggressive, insensitive, a slave to old traditions and old hang-ups. If a man wants to make a statement about himself, if he wants to wear a string of beads to say he is caring and sensitive and secure within himself, then he can today without fear of being stereotyped. These beads are my way of saying that I am *laid back*, man."

The entire conversation was far over my head. "Laid back?" I asked.

"Where have you been?" asked my friend. "For years, men have been taught that it's not okay for them to cry, it's not okay for them to enjoy flowers or to dress colorfully or to wear ornamental jewelry. Men who did that were—what was your term?—sissies. Well, we don't have to be like that anymore. Now, we can do our own things. Women really go for guys who can feel, who can share their thoughts, who like poetry and art and antiques and don't mind admitting it. It's even okay for a man to have a cat now."

I was taken aback by all this. True, I had been taught that a man was supposed to be strong and aggressive, and I had always despised cats.

I vowed to change my ways. I borrowed my friend's beads, bought a copy of Kahlil Gibran's *The Prophet*, and took a girl out on a date to the art museum and later to an antique store, where we browsed and looked at brass beds and old pictures of somebody else's grandparents. I thought that was very sensitive of me.

When we reached her house at the end of our date, she said, "I find you so comfortable to be with. You're so sensitive and you don't mind sharing your thoughts. You're so, well, *laid back.*"

I thought I spotted an opening and asked if I could spend the night with her.

"Silly boy," she said. "My cat would be so jealous."

These were trying times for me. With apologies to George Gobel, the world around me seemed to be a tuxedo and I was still a pair of brown shoes.

Leisure suits. Neck chains. Kinky. Macho. Laid back. Men crying and keeping company with cats. Everywhere I looked, there was upheaval and change. And more was on the way.

Women's stated interest in men's chest hairs, which led to the unbuttoned shirts and neck chains and beads, was followed by another shocking admission—they also enjoyed looking at our butts and seeing us in our underpants.

Let's begin with the underpants. The basic rules for men's underpants always had gone something like this:

After a boy-child passes the diaper stage, he moves into what is known as "grippers," or "jockey shorts." These shorts fit very tightly, since small boys have not yet reached the point where tight underwear can cause discomfort and migraine headaches. Before a boy's voice changes, it is perfectly okay for his jockey shorts to have pictures on them, as long as they're pictures of Army tanks or cowboys. Birds and flowers are totally unacceptable.

Once a boy reaches his teens and begins undressing in locker rooms in front of his friends, he still can wear jockey shorts, but forget the pictures of Army tanks and cowboys. Boys at this stage wear plain, white jockey shorts, but they have to be more careful about shorts that fit too snugly because of the aforementioned headaches.

Upon graduation, a young man is fully expected to change into boxer shorts. These shorts are white and they hit just above the knees. A young man should wear this type of undershorts for the remainder of his life, even is he eventually winds up with a truss underneath his clothing, too.

That's the way it used to be, back in a simpler time. Then came Jim Palmer.

Jim Palmer is a famous baseball pitcher who is quite handsome. Some advertising genius got the bright idea to take a picture of Jim Palmer in a pair of bikini-type underwear for men and put it in a lot of magazines. Men, or should I say those who do not make a habit of looking at pictures of other men in their underpants, ignored these pictures of Jim Palmer, but women didn't.

They began to say to their mates such things as "Why don't you get some sexy underwear like Jim Palmer wears?"

A lot of men went out and did that, but it posed a real problem for others. What good did it do to wear Jim Palmer underwear if you happened to look like Yogi Berra?

I didn't know what to do. I had a couple of dozen pairs of normal, white boxer shorts, and even walking past a display of Jim Palmer bikini-type underpants made me feel quite silly. My wife at the time insisted, however, that I try out a pair, so I dutifully went into the men's underwear section of a large department store.

Why do they allow women to sell men's underwear?

"Can I help you with something?" asked the girl in the underwear department. I wondered if her father knew she had this job.

"Yes," I mumbled, "I would like to buy some underwear."

"And what type would you like, sir?" she went on.

"Well," I said, "I'm not really certain. Do you have any of those like what's -his-name, the baseball player, wears?"

"Oh, you mean the Jim Palmer jockey brief. Yes, we have all colors in four sizes—Small, Medium, Large, and XLC."

"XLC?"

"Extra Large Crotch," said the salesgirl.

I thought of running out the door. I would never see the salegirl again, and I could tell my wife that when I got to the department store, there were a lot of fruity-looking characters buying Jim Palmer's underwear and I didn't want to be a part of it.

Before I could make my move, however, the salesgirl was standing in front of me with several pairs of Jim Palmer jockey briefs.

"I can see you're a little unsure, sir," she said. "Why don't you step into our dressing room and try on a pair and see how you like them?"

"Incidentally," I said," what size are these?"

"Well," said the salesgirl, "it's only a guess, but I picked Small."

When nobody was looking, I slipped out of the dressing room and left my Jim Palmer jockey briefs there. I would explain to my wife that they were all out of my size, and she would understand. She would realize that they probably didn't make many XLC's for guys, well guys like me.

"All out of Small, huh?" replied my wife.

Jim Palmer was recently released from the Baltimore Orioles and his baseball career is likely over, so I hope he'll put his pants back on and leave the rest of us alone for awhile.

The second part of the problem, as you remember, was that women enjoyed looking at men's butts. They even had calendars with pictures of naked men showing off their buns. This feminine interest in men's hindparts led to another problem regarding the wardrobe, but first some background.

Previous to the revelation that women enjoyed the aesthetic qualities of the male hindpart, men spent little time considering the shape of their hips, much less the presentation of same. They selected a pair of trousers on the basis of comfort alone. Consequently, most men walked around in baggy pants, which offered the ultimate in comfort and free movement, but which also totally veiled the male rear and suggested on some occasions that a family of gypsies had moved out of the seat.

Women's liberation came along, however, and the baggy pants industry went bust, but a boom followed in the blue jean game.

Before, only cowboys and young men under the age of seventeen had worn blue jeans. There was an obvious reason for cowboys' wearing this attire. You can get all sorts of substances on a pair of jeans, like what cows leave all over the dusty trail, and still not have to wash them for weeks at a time...especially if all the other cowboys' jeans are smelly, too.

Most little boys wanted to be just like the cowboys back then, so their mothers dressed them in jeans. I not only wanted to be a cowboy when I was a child, I was convinced I *was* one. As a matter of fact, I was convinced I was Roy Rogers, who was my favorite western star.

Before we moved to tiny Moreland, we lived in a large apartment complex in Virginia while my father soldiered. I got lost one day. I began to cry. (Cowboys never cry unless they're five and hopelessly lost and hungry and want their mothers.) A kind lady attempted to find out where I lived so she could take me home.

"What's your name, little boy?" she asked.

"Roy Rogers," I said.

She called the resident manager's office and asked where the Rogers family lived. There was no family by that name in the apartment complex.

"Are you certain your name is Roy Rogers?" she asked me again.

"Does Trigger have a long tail?" I asked her back.

Finally, the lady began calling all the apartments asking if anybody had a retarded child who thought he was Roy Rogers. Thankfully, my mother claimed me when the lady reached her.

After high school, a male was expected to step out of his blue jeans and into a pair of baggy pants. It was in this style of dress that he then would leave home for the serious effort of educating himself further, learning a trade, or joining the armed forces, which strenuously objected to any form of tight-fitting trousers since they would deter swift movement on the battlefield.

That has all changed, however. Today, men normally have a closet full of blue jeans, because nothing shows off the hips better than a pair of tight-fitting blue jeans, and they're considered appropriate attire for practically every occasion except state funerals.

Most men, raised under the old rules of loose-fitting pants, had to learn a number of new rules about buying jeans:

1. They had to remember to buy their jeans at least two inches smaller in the waist than the jeans and trousers they bought before Women's Liberation. Some jeans advertised a "skosh" more room in the seat, but I don't think they sold very well. That one little "skosh" just might be enough to cause you to go unnoticed by a gaggle of gimlet-eyed legal secretaries hip-watching during a Friday afternoon happy hour.

2. They had to remember that if they decided to bend over for any

reason while wearing tight-fitting jeans, they should take a deep breath first to avoid passing out. Rule 2-A is, if you bend over and hear a ripping sound, place both hands over your backside and run backwards towards the nearest restroom. At an outdoor function, cover and run backwards towards the nearest heavy growth of kudzu.

3. It was important to note that tight-fitting jeans could be the devil to remove from your body. Men had to remember always carry a pocketknife with them when they were wearing tight jeans, just in case it became necessary to cut them away from their bodies in an extreme emergency...such as if they were sick and tired of sleeping in them.

4. Men had to accept the fact that while they were wearing tight jeans, they absolutely had to hold their stomachs in at all times, even though doing so would cause their faces to turn red and their eyes to bug out (not to mention the possibility of swollen ankles).

It was in the late seventies that I finally relented and went out and bought my first pair of adult blue jeans. I was surprised at the varieties available. Even the noted snooty designers Bill Blass and Calvin Klein had jeans lines, which suddenly cost what a man used to pay for a Sunday suit.

I bought myself a pair of tight-fitting Kleins and wore them out of the store and headed to the nearest singles bar. I ordered a drink and made certain I kept my backside pointed toward the tables of legal secretaries sipping piña coladas, figuring the sight of my new jeans hugging closely to my hips would knock the umbrellas right out of their glasses.

Unfortunately, no action was forthcoming. A man standing next to me in a pair of tight-fitting Bill Blass jeans finally turned to me and said, "How long you been here?"

"Couple of beers," I answered.

"Me, too," he replied. "I don't think I've gotten one glance."

There was something terribly wrong here. We had both spent half a week's salary on a pair of designer jeans that we had stuffed ourselves into, and all the women who were supposed to go wild at the sight of men's hips hadn't shown the slightest interest.

"I guess it's like my old grandpa used to say," said Bill Blass. "'It don't matter what kind of rifle you have if you ain't got any ammunition to load it with.'"

I finished my beer, went home, and cut myself out of my Calvin Klein jeans. I spent the remainder of the evening attempting to learn to breathe normally again.

I have never ceased to be amazed by the lengths men will go to satisfy a feminine whim. Take aftershave lotion. God gave men Old Spice aftershave lotion, and that should have been enough. But, no. Women decided that Old Spice, which is what everybody's daddy wore, wasn't nearly the sexy aroma they wanted, and so men had another problem—What sort of aftershave should I use to set my woman's blood to boiling?

There was English Leather. You know what the sexy lady on television says about that—"My men wear English Leather...or they wear nothing at all."

I can just see it now. I go over to have dinner with her and her parents, and I show up naked as a jaybird.

"Are you crazy?" she screams at me.

"Well," I attempt to explain, "I was all out of English Leather and the stores were closed, so like you say, either I wear English Leather or I wear..."

Somebody later figured out that what a woman really wanted to smell on a man was his natural odor with a little perfume thrown in. The upshot of that revelation was something called "musk." I could never bring myself to splash anything called "musk" all over my face. It sounded too much like the way it smelled in the kitchen after I hadn't taken the garbage out for a week.

Pete Rose tried to get us back on track and away from all those exotic perfumed potions when he claimed "a man wants to smell like a man" and urged us all to buy Aqua Velva, first cousin to Old Spice. Of course, with Pete Rose's money, he could splash tobacco juice on his face and still make out.

The big question facing men today is, if I use Paco Rabanne cologne, will I score as much as the guys in their advertisements obviously do?

I never have actually smelled Paco Rabanne, but their ads, which also appear in a number of women's magazines because women are the ones who buy most of the cosmetics for men in the first place, are something else.

Get the picture: This muscular fellow is in bed and covers are all askew. It's obvious that the only thing between him and butt-naked is the sheet he has pulled up just enough to avoid embarrassing his parents, in case they happened to stumble across the ad.

He's on the telephone, talking to the woman who spent the night with him but who had to get up early for an appointment with the board of directors. She is a totally New Woman, who doesn't want children until she has been made a partner in the firm. She also is very open about her sexuality, which means she always carries an extra toothbrush in her handbag just in case.

In a Paco Rabanne ad, you read the dialogue between the man naked in the bed and the woman on the other end of the telephone. It goes something like this:

WOMAN: "You animal."

MAN: "I was just thinking about you."

WOMAN: "You beast."

MAN: "So it was good for you. I was embarrassed to ask."

WOMAN: "My toes are still tingling."

MAN: "Down, girl."

WOMAN: "What are you doing right now?"

MAN: "I'm naked under the sheets."

WOMAN: "You devil."

MAN: "Are you coming back over tonight?"

WOMAN: "Can Burl Ives sell tea?"

MAN: "I'll splash on lots of Paco Rabanne."

WOMAN: "Forget my career. Forget my partnership in the firm. I'll be right over."

MAN: "Sure you don't mind?"

WOMAN: "My mind might not be sure, you hunk, but the rest of me is."

*Paco Rabanne for men. What is remembered is up to you.*

How are men supposed to stick to something simple like Old Spice when they can pop for a little Paco Rabanne and maybe stay naked under the sheets for weeks at a time?

Sex. It's everywhere. It's in the music, it determines what clothes we wear, and even what we splash on our faces after we shave.

Do we really have it better than our parents? Sex was simple for them. All they had to do was memorize one position and remember to turn the light off.

But sex has been a whole new ball game for my generation. I'm still not certain if a *ménage à trois* is some sort of French cooking with lots of sauce or something you do naked under the sheets with a girls' volleyball team. And with my luck, about the time I find out, I'll have ulcers and will be too old for it to really matter.

# • Maybe Someday, Rainbow Stew

"We've seen the old way of life that we were raised on, and we've seen the new one that has given us ulcers; maybe we can pick the best of each and produce a world where everybody has a fair chance and an air conditioner. But salad bars will be unlawful."

For most of my adult life, the only thing that has been perfectly clear to me has been the booze I've used to steady my nerves. You name it and it has confused me, because usually I was right in the middle of an issue, leaning towards both sides.

We could start with Vietnam. I was born a patriot of patriots, and I don't give a rat's tail for the Commies, but I also didn't want to be sent off to get shot in some rice paddy, and I didn't want anybody else to, either.

And drugs. There I was, standing off to the fringes, clinging to the cold beer in my hand while others sat in a circle and passed around a marijuana cigarette and appeared to be having a wonderful time. All I could do was seek refuge with my own kind in some beer joint, playing country music and the Bowl-A-Matic machine.

We've been all over the music. I took off after Elvis, but had I known where he and his music eventually would lead—there's a rock singer today who bites the heads off bats as part of his performance—I likely would have stayed with Red Foley.

And free sex. It has its good points, but what if I get herpes?

Constant dilemma, the legacy for my generation—the In-Betweeners—is a wearisome thing, and I don't mind admitting that I'm weary of it.

God knows, I have tried my best to fit into modern life. I bought a new house a year ago, and it has a Jacuzzi in the bathroom. One simply has not arrived today unless one has a Jacuzzi (which sounds like the Italian world for getting bubbles up your butt).

I've been in my Jacuzzi twice. Once, I had hurt my back playing tennis, and the doctor had said that if I had a Jacuzzi, it would be a good idea to get in it and soak my back in the hot, bubbling water.

The problem came when I tried to get out of the Jacuzzi. My back hurt so much I couldn't lift myself out. I was rescued several hours later by sheet rock workers who had come to repair a hole in the wall of my bathroom—which was the result of the first time I got into my Jacuzzi and felt those bubbles in my rear. I thought there was something strange in the tub that wanted to make friends, and in my haste to get out, I fell and knocked a hole in the wall.

So if I really am that tired of the dilemmas of modern life, what can I do about it?

First, I have to come to grips with the fact that I soon will be forty, and it's time I stopped trying to understand all that is strange and new to me. By the time a person is forty, it's much too late to comprehend anything young people are doing or thinking, and we look silly when we try.

The best thing to do is what our parents did—write off the younger generation as totally gone to hell. If you need evidence, cite the children out in Texas who put dead bats in their mouths in an effort to emulate that nut rock singer I mentioned earlier. These children had to take rabies shots for biting bats, and our parents thought we were strange because we listened to Elvis. (I hope most parents of In-Betweeners now realize that Elvis wasn't that bad after all, compared to what is happening today. If they have, then rest well, Elvis, wherever you are; all is forgiven.)

But if kids today want to eat bats, there's nothing I can do about it, so I might as well relax and worry about something I can control. Nothing that I have control over comes to mind right off, but at least that's something else I can worry about.

After I have accepted the fact that I'm out of step with modernity, I must then look for a niche in which to crawl and rest contentedly with the idea of retirement; I'm too far gone to run in the fast lane.

I don't know if I'll ever take what seems to be a drastic step for someone who has been an urban creature for more than half his life, but I do occasionally dream of going home. Back to my roots. Back to Moreland.

Somebody once said to me, "We spend the first half of our lives trying to get away from home. We spend the second half trying to get back."

Growing up in Moreland is the primary reason I am what I am—a premature curmudgeon, longing for the simple life—and I wonder if moving back would fulfill that longing.

The boys from Moreland. Some of us got away, others didn't. Dudley Stamps is still living there. He built himself a house on the land where he was reared, and he works on cars. He steadfastly refused to budge from where he was when the changes came.

He built a stereo system in his new house that piped music into all the rooms, and he issued a dictum to his wife that never, under any circumstances, would there be anything but country music on his stereo system. He caught her disobeying his order one day—she was playing a rock 'n' roll station on the radio—and that may have been one of the things that led to their divorce. At least the man had his priorities in order.

Danny Thompson and Anthony Yeager stayed around home, too, and Clyde Elrod came back. He did just what he said he was going to do; he spent twenty years in the Navy, retired, and now drives the butane truck in Moreland. I was home for a visit not long ago, and he came by to fill my parents' tank. He told me that he used to go out on a ship for days and sit there and look out on the Indian Ocean, and all he could think about was getting back to Moreland one day.

"We didn't know how good we had it growing up," he said.

I enthusiastically concurred.

The other boys from Moreland, like me, still haven't given in to the urge to return. Bobby Entrekin has a wife and a daughter and he travels, too, so I rarely see him. I've lost track of Charlie Moore. Mike Murphy has three kids and his own business, and Worm Elrod is a hairdresser.

I suppose I also should mention Little Eddie Estes. Soon after he made that marvelous catch in centerfield to save the game against Grantville, he died in an automobile accident. He was only fourteen. His mother and daddy buried him in the Moreland Methodist cemetery, about three long fly balls from the exact spot where he made the catch.

While the rest of the world went bananas, Moreland changed very little at heart. Today, Cureton and Cole's store is boarded shut, and they're trying to refurbish the old hosiery mill and turn it into some kind of museum that reflects life in the village a hundred years ago. Moreland still respects its past, and I like that.

Steve Smith's truck stop is gone, but the interstate took most of the truck traffic anyway, and that makes Moreland even quieter. There is still no traffic light and no police department, and they still have dinner-on-the-grounds at the Methodist and Baptist churches. And you still have to drive to Luthersville in the next county to buy a bottle of whiskey. It would do me good to live someplace where the nearest bottle of whiskey is a county away.

They're still neighborly in Moreland. My Aunt Una and her husband, John, live just up the dirt road from my parents. John came down sick and they didn't know what they were going to do about plowing their garden.

"One day," my Aunt Una was telling me, "we heard this commotion out in the garden, and we looked out and there was one of our neighbors—a pilot who bought a farm down here—on his tractor plowing our garden for us. I don't know what we would have done without him."

They still plant gardens in Moreland, too, and if I lived there, there would be no reason to set foot in a McDonald's again. My Aunt Jessie, who lives on the other side of my parents' house, continues to work her own garden despite her age.

I had lunch with her recently. She served fried chicken, baked chicken, baked ham, cornbread dressing, butter beans, field peas, green beans, fried okra, sliced home grown tomatoes, creamed corn, mashed potatoes with gravy, several varieties of cake and three pecan pies she had baked herself, and a large container of iced tea. We sat under a big tree outside and feasted upon her offerings, and there was peace in the moment.

But even if I never take the final plunge and move back home, I know that Moreland is there, mostly yet unspoiled, and that settles me when I'm caught in a traffic jam or waiting for a light to change in the city, as I stand next to a kid with a ghetto blaster on his shoulder, beating out sounds to have a nervous breakdown by. In Moreland, the music you hear is that of one of the church choirs, drifting out the open windows on a soft, still Sunday morning.

And although I remain fearful that the world eventually will go crazy enough to spin off its axis and fly into space somewhere, there are, in fact, occasional glimpses of hope that manifest themselves.

We have a popular, conservative president who once played cowboy roles in the movies. Sigma Pi, my old fraternity at Georgia, was kicked off campus in the seventies, primarily because of drug use in the chapter. It currently is making a comeback. There was even a recent letter to the editor of the Atlanta papers written by a disgruntled University of Georgia student. His complaint was that the university faculty was too liberal for the mostly conservative student body.

I read somewhere that sales on white socks are up twenty percent. Pickup truck sales have been on the rise for years, and more and more bars are selling beer in longneck bottles. There's a joint I go to in Atlanta where they have an all country jukebox, including a complete study in George Jones, and, right there on Peachtree Street in trendy Buckhead, the place is packed every night.

Tobacco chewing and snuff-dipping are in style again, and ridership on America's passenger trains is at an all-time high. There was a recent month in which there were four separate passenger train accidents, including one in New York where two trains collided head-on. One person was killed and a hundred were injured, and people who prefer planes made a big deal of it. But if I'm going to be in an accident while traveling, I still would prefer it to be on a train. Let two jets run together and see how many walk away.

Traditional clothing is in again. In fact, you're called a "preppie" if you wear button-down collars today. But I still contend there would be less crime and craziness in this country if everybody dressed nicely. You never hear of anybody robbing a liquor store dressed in a Polo shirt and a pair of khakis and Weejuns with no socks. Check police records if you don't believe me.

Some changes, like air conditioning, have been good for us all. Even people who live in the most rural areas of the country have air conditioning now. I have an acquaintance in a small town who sells air conditioning. He told me about getting a telephone call at his office from a lady who lived so far back in the country that the sun went down between her house and the road.

"She wanted to know what kind of air conditioners I had and what they cost. I was telling her about one air conditioner with this many BTUs and another air conditioner with that many BTUs. When I finished, she said, 'All I want is an air conditioner that will cool a b-u-t-t as big as a t-u-b.'"

Still, if we don't someday cut back on radical change and unchecked progress, we may all get our b-u-t-ts blown away or replaced by robots. Or else we might end up taking off all our clothes and squatting naked in trees, like Crazy Melvin, not worrying about it.

Maybe it will be us, the In-Betweeners, who finally make some sense out of the world again. We're still young enough I have the energy to do it, and, as we get older, perhaps we will have the wisdom, too. We've seen the old way of life that we were reared in, and we've seen the new one that has given us ulcers; maybe we can pick the best of each and produce a world where everybody has a fair chance and an air conditioner. But salad bars will be unlawful.

And if we're able to do that—if we're able to lead the way out of the wilderness of frightening modernity and back into the land of simplicity and contentment that we knew as children—then having lived with the dilemmas will have been worth it. Somebody has to do something before the Democrats nominate Phil Donahue for president and he up and picks Billie Jean King as his running mate.

But until that day comes, play me the old songs, bring around my old friends, keep the beer cold, and constantly remind me to cling to the immortal words of the man who sings now in the void left by Elvis, Merle Haggard:

*"One of these days,*
*When the air clears up*
*And the sun comes shinin' through,*
*We'll all be drinkin' that free Bubble-Up*
*And eatin' that Rainbow Stew."*

Shoot Low, Boys: They're Ridin' Shetland Ponies *is a book about heroes. Lewis Grizzard goes back to John Wayne's Rooster Cogburn for his first definition of heroism, and then develops his own personal concept of modern-day grit.* Shoot Low, Boys *explores the everyday heroism of everyday people, including those close to him like his grandmother and mother, and those he admired from a greater distance like Dr. Barney Clark, the first human recipient of an artificial heart. Grizzard also delves into a variety of experiences in modern life that test the patience and sanity of everyone, like selling a house, buying lingerie, and traveling, especially overseas. Grizzard's look at the real meaning of true grit and the unsung heroes of our era makes* Shoot Low, Boys *both a hilarious and touching end to this compilation of his early work.*

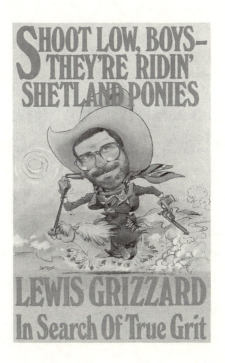

**1985**

# •Never Go Camping with a Man Who Drinks Whiskey Sours

"As for myself, I'm a beer drinker. We are usually honest, straightforward people. We also are usually kind and quite sentimental and will get cryin'-about-our-daddies drunk with one another. That's just before we destroy the establishment in which we're drinking because somebody made an offhand remark about Richard Petty or the memory of Patsy Cline."

One of the things John Wayne had going for him in *True Grit* (and in real life, for that matter) was that he looked the part. Tall, strong, ruggedly handsome and tough to the bone. The way he walked, the way he talked, the clothes he wore—all these things added to his aura.

The same was true of another of my childhood heroes, Superman. When he was dressed as Clark Kent, mild-mannered reporter for a large metropolitan newspaper—black-rimmed glasses, white shirt, striped tie, blue suit and wing-tipped shoes—nobody paid him any attention. Certainly not Lois Lane. But the minute he switched into that tight-fitting Superman costume and started leaping tall buildings in a single bound, Lois was on him like bark on a tree.

So maybe "the look" is part of the recipe for true grit. I'm not arguing that clothes make the man, but I've dated enough women hiding vast quantities of themselves under muumuus to know that diversionary tactics can work.

It's easy enough to chronicle the traditional manly characteristics which the Duke embodied. For one, he always seemed to have a couple of days worth of stubble on his chin and a little hair hanging over his collar.

I have more than a couple of days worth of stubble; I've got a beard. I decided to grow it several years ago after someone called me "fishface." I think the implication was that I have a weak chin. I found that a beard made me look more mature and even gave me an air of pseudo-sophistication. I liked it.

So I took the look one step further and started smoking cigars. They, too, I reasoned, made me look mature and urbane. One day while smoking my cigar, I accidentally knocked the fire off the end. I didn't immediately see where it fell, but I soon discovered that a burning beard gives off a terrible odor.

I gave up cigars after that frightening experience and started carrying a copy of the *Wall Street Journal* under my arm. It gave me the same aura of authority and, whereas a cigar lasts no more than an hour or so, I could carry the same *Wall Street Journal* around for a week or more before it started turning yellow and I had to buy another.

Anyway, I have the beard, and I also have the hair over the collar. In fact, I've been wearing my hair long for years. It's like a muumuu for my ears.

I never noticed that I had big ears until I was in the fourth grade and Alvin Bates pointed them out to me. "Your ears poke way out," he said. I looked in a mirror and discovered that for once in his life he wasn't lying. I also had a lot of freckles on my nose, and when I smiled I bore an amazing resemblance to Howdy Doody, the late puppet. I hoped that no one else noticed the similarity.

"How's Clarabell?" asked Alvin Bates in a loud voice the next morning when I walked into class. That was only the beginning of the abuse I took from my classmates.

"Mind putting your head down on your desk?" the girl who sat behind me asked one day during an arithmetic lesson.

I didn't have any better sense at the time than to ask her why.

"Because, Howdy," she said to the delight of the jackals sitting around her, "I can't see the blackboard for your ears."

I tried everything to make my ears grow closer to my head. At night I slept with a rubber band around my head to hold my ears in. Can you imagine how much it hurt when the rubber band broke in the middle of the night? I even tried gluing my ears to my head. Inevitably one of them would come unglued, leaving me looking like I was giving signals to a train.

My only salvation came years later when long hair, fashionably trimmed over the ears, came into style. But even that caused me some trauma.

You will remember that my father was a military man and consequently was not fond of long hair. Many times his cohorts told me the story of how he dealt with a young recruit sporting more than regulation locks:

"We had some new recruits come in to Fort Benning," the story began, "and they sent the Captain, your old man, out to look them over and get them checked out for their first day on post. He came to this little ol' skinny boy with hair down over his eyes and way down on the bottom of his neck. That wouldn't be anything today, but back then he looked real strange.

"Your daddy looked him up and down real slow and then made a horrible face and said, 'Son, as soon as I dismiss you, I want you to go over to the hospital and check yourself in. Have the doctors give you a thorough going over.'

"The kid said to your daddy, 'Do you think there's something wrong with me, sir?'

"Your daddy said, 'Yes, indeed, soldier. I think beyond a shadow of a doubt that if the doctors look close enough, somewhere on you they will find a vagina.'"

Even after all these years, I can handle the guilt better than my uncovered ears.

Another thing common to men like Rooster Cogburn is that they're bad to drink or chew or do both. You can tell a lot about people by noticing what they drink. For instance, I was in a restaurant recently when a man walked in and asked the hostess, "How long before I can have a table?"

"About fifteen minutes," the hostess said.

"Good," the man answered. "That'll give me time for a whiskey sour at the bar."

I can't explain why, but a whiskey sour is a drink for a man whose mother made him practice piano a lot when he was a kid. A man who drinks whiskey sours also probably throws a baseball like a girl—limp-wristed. A man who drinks whiskey sours and then eats that silly little cherry they put in the bottom probably has a cat or a poodle for a pet. In other words, I wouldn't go on a camping trip with a man who drinks whiskey sours.

Scotch drinkers are aggressive. They order like they're Charles Bronson trying to have a quick shot before returning to the subway to kill a few punks and thugs.

"What'll you have, sir?" asks the bartender.

"Cutty. Water. Rocks. Twist," growls the Scotch drinker. I think maybe Scotch drinkers wear their underwear too tight.

You have to watch people who drink vodka or gin. "Anybody who drinks see-through whiskey," an old philosopher once said, "will get crazy." Indeed. Vodka and gin drinkers are the type who leave the house to get a loaf of bread, drop by the bar for just one, and return home six weeks later. With the bread.

I wouldn't go on a camping trip with anyone who drinks vodka or gin, either. They're the types who would invite snakes, raccoons and bears over for cocktails and then wind up getting into an argument about tree frogs.

Bourbon drinkers never grow up. Eight out of ten started drinking bourbon with Coke in school and still have a pair of saddle oxfords in the closet. Bourbon drinkers don't think they've had a good time unless they get sick and pass out under a coffee table.

Then there are the white wine drinkers. Never get involved in any way with them. They either want to get married, sell you a piece of real estate, or redecorate your house.

As for myself, I'm a beer drinker. We're usually honest, straightforward people. We also are usually kind and quite sentimental and will get cryin'-about-our-daddies drunk with one another. That's just before we destroy the establishment in which we're drinking because somebody made an offhand remark about Richard Petty or the memory of Patsy Cline.

Never go camping with a beer drinker, either. We're really no fun unless there's a jukebox around, and we belch a lot, which might frighten the snakes, raccoons, bears, and tree frogs.

I occasionally get an urge to chew tobacco, and snuff-dipping is a part of my heritage, but I have a distinct problem with both. I'm talking about the mess they make.

There used to be two popular commercials promoting snuff, one featuring former professional football player Walt ("Just a pench between yo' cheek and gum") Garrison and another starring the famous fiddle player and singer Charlie Daniels. The commercials always showed these fellows smiling as they snuffed up, but they never showed them spitting. If you dip, you spit. If you dip and don't spit, you have swallowed your snuff and soon will die a slow, agonizing death unless somebody has a stomach pump handy.

My grandmother was a snuff user. She used to send me to the store to buy her "medicine," as she called it. Then she would sit for hours with her Bible in her lap and a dip behind her lip. I knew it wasn't medicine. If it had been, no one would have kept it in their mouth that long.

One afternoon while returning from the store with my grandmother's "medicine," I decided to sample it. The convulsions began immediately. I managed to spit some of it out, but most of it went in my nose and eyes. The remaining portion I swallowed. If there had been a doctor nearby, I would have been pronounced dead on arrival at home. Month-old lettuce looked better than I did.

If there were truth in advertising, manufacturers of snuff would be required to print a warning on the side of cans: "Dip or chew if you want, but know that you're going to have to spit every eight seconds or so and probably will get it all over your shoes."

Not only do those snuff commercials fail to show people spitting, they also never show them with spittle curling out of the corners of their mouths. "Dip or chew if you want," another warning should say, "but be prepared to look like you've been eating mud."

I have a friend who has been chewing tobacco for years. Like all other chewers, he spits a lot and juice runs out the sides of his mouth. His wife tried to get him to stop because she was offended by the little spit cups she found all over the house. There's nothing more unappealing than a cup of day-old tobacco spit.

Finally she said to him, "That's it. I've had it. Either the chewing tobacco goes or I go."

"Honey," my friend replied, "I don't have but one vice. I don't stay out drunk, I don't chase women and I'm kind to children, old people and dogs. But my daddy chewed and his daddy before him, and chewing is in my blood. Asking me to give it up is like asking a dog to stop licking his privates. I couldn't stop even if I wanted to."

His wife studied on this statement for a few months and said, "OK, if it means that much to you, I suppose I can live with it."

Soon afterwards they were celebrating their wedding anniversary. My friend's wife gave him a leather pouch for storing his chewing tobacco and he gave her the promise that he'd go outside whenever he needed to spit.

That compromise took guts on both their parts—so much, in fact, that I was inspired to write a poem about it. It went like this:

*True love.*
*True grit.*
*You need 'em both*
*When you've got to spit.*
*Ptui.*

Another ingredient of true grit, judging from most of The Duke's movies, could be body odor. Think about it: Except for when he wrestled some galoot into the river and knocked him senseless, did you ever see that pilgrim bathe? No, sir. The Duke liked to smell like a man... or at least like a man who had been riding the range for a month without a bath.

Back before air conditioning became one of the elements essential to life, it was perfectly all right to sweat a little and to emit an aromatic scent. Everybody did. Your mother sweated over a hot stove. Your father sweated at work and then came home and sat around in his underwear and sweated some more. At the end of a long day, nobody asked, "Where did you park your goats?" Nobody said, "Isn't it about time you looked for a reliable underarm deodorant?"

Today, sweat stains under the arms are considered only slightly less offensive than Joan Rivers. They can lead to the loss of a big account: "Sorry, Wilson, but we're going to have to find ourselves a new boy. Those perspiration stains on your shirt are a disgrace to the firm." Or to the loss of a lover: "I'll always love you, Marvin, but you've got the Okefenokee Swamp under your arms." Or even to the breakup of a family: "I'm filing for divorce, Donna. Those underarm stains on your tennis blouse are ruining the children's chances at a full and happy life."

Mandatory air conditioning not only did away with underarm sweat stains, it also led to the demise of a great tradition: the paddle fan. In the little Methodist church in my hometown, there were always Cokesbury hymnals and paddle fans along the back of each pew. The fans generally were provided by either a funeral home or an ambitious politician, with their message on one side—"Arnold's Funeral Home/ Free Parking" or "Vote for Grover (Shorty) Turnipseed, County Commissioner"—and a four-color biblical scene on the other side (usually the Last Supper).

It wasn't necessary to listen to the minister's words to know whether or not he was reaching back for one of those you-had-better-change-your-evil-ways sermons. All you had to do was watch the congregation. The faster they fanned themselves, the closer to home the preacher was hitting.

The mere mention of the evils of alcohol was certain to speed the fanning strokes, and when the minister began to describe the warm climate that one who imbibed could expect at his final address, a draft no manner of air conditioner could match would roar through the sanctuary off those paper fans.

If I were a minister today, I would use a two-prong attack to challenge my backsliding flock. First, I would turn off the air conditioning some hot Sunday morning, and then I would explain the major difference between the two possible destinations that awaited them: hell for companionship, perhaps; heaven for its climate. Then I would quietly take my seat and let them sweat out their decisions without benefit of paddle fans. Now, that's the sort of situation that develops true grit.

Our preoccupation with smelling any way except natural doesn't end with air conditioning and deodorant, of course. "Is your mouthwash doing the job?" asked a commercial on television the other night. I don't know the answer to that. I brush my teeth every day whether they need it or not, and I even gargle on occasion. But how do I know if my mouth has that awful medicine smell they were talking about on TV?

I can hear my friends now: "He's a decent guy, but somebody really ought to tell him he has medicine mouth."

The same is true of shampoo. According to current commercials, if the shampoo you're using doesn't clean your hair, remove all dandruff, and leave your hair bright and shiny and full of body and smelling like a flower shop, people might not allow you in the same room with their children. You could infect the little boogers.

The new shampoos, of course, are highly scented, and one even leaves your hair smelling like apricots. Here's a hint: If you happen to be a man, never walk into a truck stop with your hair smelling like apricots. Someone likely will make fruit salad out of your head.

Come to think of it, that's probably the kind of shampoo that Lucky Ned Pepper was using, and that's why the marshall was so riled. That and the fact that just before their big shootout, Ned yelled across to Rooster Cogburn, "Hey, big guy, what's your sign?"

Another quality I associate with The Duke is that he was always friendly with his critters. His horse loved him. His cattle loved him. And in several movies he had a dog by his side. A man needs a good dog— one who'll fetch a stick and lick his hand. Don't forget what Bullet did for Roy Rogers and what Rin Tin Tin did for Sergeant Preston.

I'm not talking about those highfaluting purebreds who have been pampered by their owners and registered with the American Kennel Club. I don't like pampered children, and I don't like pampered dogs. I want a dog with character and personality, one who had to turn over a trash can once in a while just to keep food in his stomach. And I like a dog who knows enough about where puppies come from that he can choose his own mate and take care of business without waiting for some high-hatted human to "arrange" a canine tête-à-tête for him.

Allow me to explain the types of dogs that I like and probably the kind The Duke liked, too:

- YARD DOGS—A yard dog, usually found in the rural South, is a likable sort who hangs around the back door waiting for table scraps and who crawls under trucks to get in the shade on hot days. Yard dogs are recognizable by the oil and grease on their backs and by the humble way they walk sideways toward the individual calling them.

- HOG DOGS—These are fat little dogs who come from a union of Lord-knows-what and will eat anything that is put before them. They will lick the pan clean and beg for more. In rare cases, these dogs have been known to suck eggs. On the positive side of the ledger, such dogs make the expense of a garbage disposal unnecessary.

- LAP DOGS—These are very loving dogs who crave attention and leap onto your lap and lick your face and shed all over the sofa. They especially enjoy lying on their backs and kicking their legs back and forth while you scratch their bellies. I had a great lap dog once. My wife used to scratch the dog's belly for hours. When I asked her to do the same for me, she called her mother and told her I was perverted.

- A. J. FOYT DOGS—These dogs enjoy standing on the side of the road and racing with cars when they drive by. Every neighborhood has at least one. The problem with such dogs is that they tend to become frustrated after never being able to outrun passing cars, so they resort to gnawing the tires on your car when it's parked in the driveway. They also tend to have short life spans, because sooner or later they catch one of those cars.

- SHOE DOGS—These are dogs with a shoe fetish. Leave a pair of shoes out one night and by morning they'll have them chewed back to the raw material stage. Never take a shoe dog into a Gucci store; you could be bankrupt within minutes. Regional variations of this dog will chew eyeglasses, leather-bound books, remote control devices, and Tupperware.

Finally, one of The Duke's most obvious characteristics, and an essential element, it seems to me, of true grit, was his self-sufficiency. He didn't need nobody for nothing.

I've always tried to emulate John Wayne in that regard. I've tried to learn to feed myself, clothe myself, and fix leaky pipes. After all, you never know when your wife may leave and take your dog with her.

The first thing a breathing, self-sufficient male has to learn to do is feed himself. I'm not talking about eating out or ordering pizza. There was a time when I ordered out for pizza so many times that the delivery boy started getting phone calls and mail at my house. But that's cheating; self-sufficiency means doing it yourself.

So, armed with determination and an unused kitchen in a new house, I set out to cook for myself. The first thing I did was buy one of those amazing food processors. "This food processor is state of the art," said the saleslady. "You can make your own mayonnaise with it."

Why would anybody want to make their own mayonnaise, I wondered, when the Hellman's people are perfectly willing to do it for them? Self-sufficiency, I answered.

The next morning I decided to make myself a hearty omelette. I had never made one before, but I knew I needed at least eggs, onions, tomatoes, ham, and cheese. First I decided to chop the onion in my new food processor. In less than ten seconds, I had a food processor full of onion juice. I have no idea what happened to the onion itself.

I immediately deleted onions from the recipe and proceeded. Next I put a piece of uncooked ham in my microwave oven and set the dial for five minutes. When I returned with the morning paper under my arm, the ham looked like Sherman had passed through Atlanta again. I mean, to a crisp.

Not to worry. Ham is high in cholesterol and unnecessary for a good omelette anyway. Remembering my experience with the onion in the food processor, I decided to slice the tomato by hand. Meanwhile, I put the cheese in the microwave to soften it.

When I had stopped the bleeding on my first two fingers, I checked the cheese in the microwave. That afternoon, it took the Roto-Rooter man only forty minutes to get the cheese unstuck from the sides of the oven.

I judiciously decided to forget about the omelette and simply have scrambled eggs with fresh orange juice. If the food processor would turn a fresh onion into onion juice, I reasoned it would do the same thing to an orange. I was correct. In seconds I had fresh orange juice. It tasted terrible, however. I later figured that maybe I should have peeled the orange.

I still had the eggs. The part that didn't stick to the bottom of the pan tasted like Silly Putty, so I threw the entire mess into my new garbage disposal which promptly clogged.

I waited until the pizza place opened and ordered a medium with everything except anchovies. It came with anchovies anyway, so I scraped them off the top of my pizza and electrocuted them in my microwave oven. I felt momentarily vindicated—after all, the microwave did what I intended it to do—but I felt far from self-sufficient.

That evening while watching television, I saw a commercial for a book that promised to save me hundreds of dollars a year in home repair and improvement bills. If I ordered one of these books, the announcer said, I would be able to fix my plumbing and even build myself a new patio.

No I wouldn't. I don't care how many of those books I read. I can't build or repair anything. A hammer is high technology to me.

When I was a kid, my mother bought me an erector set. I read the instructions and tried to build a crane. "Oh, look," my mother exclaimed when I finished. "You've built a 1948 DeSoto with both doors missing."

I was so inept they wouldn't allow me to play with the garden hose. "Get away from that hose," my mother would say. "You don't know nothing about machinery."

I carried this lack of knowledge into high school, where I enrolled in shop class in an effort to improve myself. As my term project, I decided to build a chair.

"What is it?" asked the shop teacher at the end of the quarter.

"It's a chair," I said.

"Looks more like a wooden model of a 1948 DeSoto with both doors missing to me," he said.

As an adult, I've always had the same problem, particularly with automobiles. "What seems to be the problem with your car?" the auto mechanic asks me.

"It's broken," I answer.

He opens the hood and looks inside at all that infernal wiring and all those other doflatchies and what's-its that make a car run. "Here's your problem," he says. "Your lolabridgelator isn't gee-hawing with your double-low, E-flat commodgelator."

What does that mean? And how did he learn that?

Around the house I'm equally confused. When I moved into a new house and tried to take a shower, there was no hot water. I called the plumber. "Here's your problem," he said. "The letters on your shower knobs are wrong. The 'H' is on the cold knob and the 'C' is on the hot knob."

It cost me nearly two hundred dollars to have the plumber move the knobs on my pipes so I would have hot water when I turned the "H" knob.

I did think I could at least build a stand for my mailbox at the new house. I went out and bought lumber and nails and bolts. I now have the only mailbox stand in town that looks like a 1948 DeSoto with the doors missing.

Finally I did find one thing mechanical that I could fix when it broke. I can stop a commode from making that annoying sound it makes sometimes after you flush it. What you do is lift the lid off the top of the commode and fiddle with the rubber dohickey until the sound stops.

Try finding that kind of information in a stupid book.

My last attempt at self-sufficiency almost proved fatal. I had a bad case of the flu, but I resolved to lick it myself without running to the doctor to have him laugh at me. Real men stick it out.

I felt worse than a five-eyed goat in a sandstorm. I was so sick my toenails turned black. I couldn't breathe, I couldn't eat, and my tongue itched. I turned to would-be friends for help and advice.

"Here's what you do," one said confidently. "You pour a glass full of bourbon and then you take a tablespoon of sugar. You eat the sugar and chase it with the glass of bourbon and then go to bed. You'll feel great the next morning."

He was partially right. I felt great while I was in the coma caused by the sugar and bourbon. When I came out of it, however, I felt just as bad as I did before.

Somebody else told me to eat lots of mustard. "It's an old custom in my family. A cup of mustard a day will cure anything."

Anything, that is, except the flu. Eating a cup of mustard without hot dogs will make your ears water.

The next advice I got was to eat honey and chase it with a heavy dose of castor oil. "Honey and castor oil will purify you and cleanse all the poison from your body," I was told.

Maybe so, but eating honey and chasing it with a heavy-duty dose of castor oil also will keep you from sitting in one place for more than five minutes for days. Captured enemy spies were threatened with the same treatment during World War II by Allied interrogators. It always worked.

Still another friend suggested that an afternoon in a sauna would be just the thing to put me back in the pink. "You get into a sauna for about an hour," said the friend, "and then you come out and drink a strong vodka tonic. Go back into the sauna for another hour and then come out and drink two vodka tonics. You return to the sauna for a third hour, then come out and finish the bottle of vodka."

"Sounds great," I said. "A sauna should really help me."

"You kiddin'? Saunas are awful for a man in your condition, but after a bottle of vodka, who cares?"

Chicken soup was the final suggestion. "Do I put vodka or castor oil in it?" I asked sheepishly.

"No, silly. Chicken soup by itself has tremendous curative powers."

I ate so much chicken soup that I had the urge to go peck corn, but I was still too sick to get off my tail feathers and go outside.

Eventually I cured myself by doing what any real man would do in a similar situation: I pulled the covers up over my head, whined, and felt sorry for myself. In a couple of days, I was fine. A victory for self-sufficiency.

So is it the stubbly beard, the long hair, drinking and chewing, sweating and stinking, loving dogs and being self-sufficient that gives a person true grit?

There must be more to it than that....

# •Sinning and Grinning and Knowing the Difference

"My grandfather also didn't like it when younger preachers used note cards to deliver their sermons. 'They ought to get it straight from the Lord,' he said many times. 'Politicians use notes.'"

I grew up hearing that good things come to those who love the Lord; the Moreland, Georgia, Methodist Church was deeply and comfortably seated in the traditional interpretation of The Word. But religion, like so many other things, isn't as simple as it used to be. Nowadays the good guys sometimes wear black and white striped hats instead of just one or the other.

Almost every day in the mail I receive a letter from some television evangelist asking me for a donation to help buy a new truck for his television equipment or to pay off the debt for the new gymnasium at New Testament University. The implication is that if I don't send them the cash, I'm on the express train for hell.

Will I end up down there with Hitler and Attila the Hun and Bonnie and Clyde just because I didn't send them five bucks for a new wrestling mat? Then again, is hell actually *down* there?

"Can you dig your way to hell?" I asked the preacher when I was a kid.

"Guess you can," he said, "but I can tell you how to get there a lot quicker."

Frankly, thinking about hell scares the you-know-where-out of me. I'd much rather think about heaven. Just the other day my mail included a pamphlet entitled, "Heaven: Are You Eligible?" I took the test and scored "too close to call."

With that kind of rating, I pay close attention to all those groups who predict the coming of Judgment Day. If some guy says he has it on good authority that the end of the world is due on October 11, then I'm particularly careful that day not to do anything awful, like telling big lies, attending an adult movie or coveting my neighbor's new Porche.

Otherwise, can you imagine your chances of getting aboard the glory train when the first question they ask you at judgment is, "For starters, what did you do today?"

"W-w-w-well, f-f-first I lied to my boss about having to go to the doctor and I went instead to see *Flesh Dance* at the Port Palace. Then I went home and kicked the tires on my '73 Ford wagon because that's what I'm stuck with when Thorndike across the street has a new Porsche."

Take a seat, boy. The southbound leaves in just a few minutes.

I know in my heart that most of these forecasts are poppycock, but my old-fashioned upbringing always keeps me just a little uneasy. Remember, everybody thought Columbus was nuts when he bought a round-trip ticket. You just never know.

That's why I started early in life being careful not to get caught in mid-sin at the precise moment of His return. I remember my first beer. I tried to chug it down but succeeded only in gagging myself.

"What's your hurry?" asked my companion in evil.

"Beer is better when you drink it fast," I answered between coughs.

Truth is, I just wanted to finish that beer quickly so I could throw the can away and get rid of the evidence in case the Second Coming were to occur in the next five to ten minutes.

I guess it is possible to overreact to these predictions. Anytime I hear another Judgment Day date, I'm reminded of the story my grandfather used to tell about an Elmer Gantry-type preacher who came through town with his tent.

"The end is close at hand, my children," the preacher screamed one night. About that time, a small boy who had just been given a toy trumpet for his birthday walked past the tent and gave his new horn a mighty toot.

The congregation panicked and bolted out of the tent. The evangelist grabbed the cash box and cut down the street at full gallop. The little boy, wondering where everybody was headed, followed the preacher.

The preacher ran faster and faster, afraid to look back, but the little boy matched him step for step, still tooting on his new horn. Finally the preacher stopped, whipped out a switchblade and said, "Watch it, Gabe, or I'll cut you!"

My grandfather wouldn't have cared much for today's big time television preachers. In his oft-stated opinion, preachers were supposed to marry folks, preach funerals, mow the grass around the church and administer to the needs of the flock (that meant consoling the poor soul who lost his job, whose wife ran off, and whose trailer burned down all in the same week). Our preacher even used to knock down the dirt dobbers' nests in the windows of the sanctuary so the inhabitants wouldn't bother the worshippers while he was trying to run the devil out of town on Sunday mornings.

Do you suppose that Oral Roberts or Jerry Falwell ever knocked down any dirt dobbers' nests?

My grandfather also didn't like it when younger preachers used note cards to deliver their sermons. "They ought to get it straight from the Lord," he said many a time. "Politicians use notes."

The preacher at Moreland Methodist when I was growing up suited my grandfather just fine. He drove an old car. He had only one suit. He did the yard work around the church, didn't use note cards, and always attempted to answer the questions of a twelve-year-old boy when things didn't add up. Once he even preached a funeral for a dog because that little boy, who loved the dog very much, asked him to.

What would Pat Robertson say over a dog?

What bothers me today is that for every glamour boy of the pulpit, there are thousands out there who tackle the devil daily, one-on-one, with little or no audience, against long odds, and occasionally on an empty stomach.

God bless them. And God, please don't let my grandfather—I know he's around there somewhere—find out that we've got preachers down here today who use cue cards and hang out with politicians.

I had a dream about all this the other night. Maybe it was my grandfather passing along a little inside information. This is how it went:

God called in the angel who is in charge of keeping an eye on what's going on in the United States. "What's all this fussing about religion and politics? I thought I had Ben Franklin and his friends work out the separation of church and state a couple of weeks ago," God said.

"Actually," said the angel, "it's been a couple of weeks heaven time, but to folks on earth it's been more than two hundred years. But every so often, they decide to argue it again."

"Who started it this time?"

"I suppose it was Jerry Falwell and the Moral Majority," answered the angel.

"Jerry who and the Moral what?"

"Jerry Falwell and the Moral Majority. Falwell is a television evangelist and he heads a fundamentalist organization called the Moral

Majority. They support President Reagan because they think you are a Republican."

"Whatever gave them an idea like that?" asked God.

"They think you sent President Reagan, a Republican, to save the morals of the country because he believes in a lot of the same things as they do."

"For instance?"

"Well, President Reagan believes in prayer in public schools, and so does the Moral Majority."

"So what's the big deal? I get thousands of prayers a day from students in public schools. Here, look at this one that came in yesterday. Pretty creative for a tenth grader:

*O Lord, hear my anxious plea.*
*Algebra is killing me.*
*I know not of 'x' or 'y,'*
*And probably won't until the day I die.*
*Please, Lord, help me at this hour*
*As I take my case to the highest power.*
*I care not for fame or loot,*
*Just help me find one square root.*

*Latin and Grammar are also trouble.*
*Guide me through this daily double.*
*And, Lord, please let me see*
*One passing mark in Chemistry.*

*Lord, why am I such a dope in school?*
*My teachers think I'm such a fool.*
*One said, 'Son, you're a horrid flop*
*You bent the saw and failed at shop.'*
*My days in class are filled with remorse.*
*I can't even pass the easiest course.*
*I hunkered down and bowed my neck,*
*But I burnt the cake and flagged Home Ec.*

*In English Lit, I studied hard*
*And read all the words of the Bard.*

*But my mind is like a hateful Judas.*
*It couldn't recall, 'Et tu, Brutus?'*

*Lord, will there ever be*
*A tougher subject than History?*
*Into the past I steadfastly delve,*
*From Plymouth Rock to 1812.*
*I learn of all those patriotic folk,*
*From John Q. Adams to James K. Polk.*
*But test time comes and I fall on my tail.*
*Was it Patrick Henry or Nathan Hale?*

*Lord, must I offer an apology*
*For three times failing Biology?*
*Why is it I'm in such a fog*
*Concerning the innards of a frog?*
*I push and strive and strain and grope*
*To come to terms with the microscope.*
*Lord, please forgive my derision,*
*But who gives a hoot for cellular division?*

*Lord, I wish that I could vanish*
*When the teacher calls on me in Spanish.*
*And I promise, it's a cinch,*
*I'll never learn a word of French.*

*Down in gym I take PE.*
*Calisthenics will be the death of me.*
*I have all the grace of a mop.*
*I made an 'F' in side straddle hop.*

*Lord, is there anything I can't flub?*
*Will I ever be in Beta Club?*
*I have never found the key to knowledge,*
*And my folks want me to go to college.*
*Oh, such a thing I constantly dread.*
*I'd as soon join the Marines instead.*
*Lord, please give me a sign*

*That you've been listening all this time.*
*If you will help, I'll give my all,*
*And won't even chew gum in study hall.*
*Please lead me out of this constant coma,*
*And give me a chance at my diploma.*
*Let others fight for church and state.*
*I pray only to graduate. Amen.*

"Now, that's a prayer worthy of my time," said God. "But apparently that's not good enough for this Falwell fellow. Tell me more about him."

"Well, he has his own television show."

"When does he visit the sick?"

"He doesn't have time for that. If he's not preaching on the air, he's busy fund raising for his ministry or else he's on one of those news shows like, 'This Week With David Brinkley,' telling people where you stand on this and that."

"Just what I needed," said God, "another spokesman." God thought for a moment and then said to the angel, "I want you to do something for me. I want you to deliver a few messages. First, tell both sides that I don't want to be any part of their political squabble. Their forefathers had the good sense to leave me out of politics, and I don't see why they can't.

"Also, tell Reagan to forget about school prayer for awhile and instead find a way to talk to the Russians before they find a way to destroy what I've created. Then tell that Falwell fellow to stop using my name to boost his television ratings and stop trying to run the country from his pulpit. Can you handle all that?" God asked the angel.

"Yes, ma'am," the angel replied.

Apparently that message I dreamed hasn't been delivered quite yet, because the Moral Majority is still busy trying to convince us that they have all the answers. Me, I'm more confused than ever. It's gotten to the point that I'm not sure I know sin when I see it. Or hear it. According to the Moral Majority, music is one of the major mediums of the devil today, and nowhere is the temperature hotter than in country music.

I'll be the first to admit that some questionable lyrics have sneaked into country music in recent years, but are the dials "down there" really tuned to WSM? In an attempt to get this disturbing issue cleared up, I contacted Mrs. Debbie Sue Ann Betty Jo Jenkins of Blue Ball, Arkansas. She's the Moral Majority's expert on the state of country music.

"May I call you Debbie Sue Ann Betty Jo?" I asked when I reached her on the phone.

"Call me anything but 'Barracuda,'" she replied. "That's what Conway Twitty called me when I tried to stop his show in Little Rock."

"You tried to stop the Conway Twitty show?"

"He was singing that trashy song about meeting a woman in a bar who was wearing tight britches," Mrs. Jenkins explained.

I know the song in question, entitled "Tight-fittin' Jeans," and I suppose it is a little suggestive. I asked Mrs. Jenkins which part of the song offended her most.

"The part where the woman tells Conway Twitty, 'Pardner, there's a tiger in these tight-fittin' jeans.'"

I quickly realized that Debbie Sue Ann Betty Jo, Mrs. Jenkins, was a bit of a tiger herself. Anybody who would try to stop Conway Twitty as he groaned to his legion of fans is not the sort of person to be taken lightly.

"What other songs offend the Moral Majority?" I asked.

"Anything by Barbara Mandrell," she said.

Barbara Mandrell a musical filth peddler? I couldn't believe it.

"Imagine such perversion as inviting a man to eat crackers in bed with you in a song," explained Mrs. Jenkins, referring of course to Ms. Mandrell's hit song, "You Can Eat Crackers in My Bed Anytime." She continued, "Decent people would never do such a thing. Beds are for sleeping on and nothing else."

"What does Mr. Jenkins think about that?" I asked.

"He doesn't even like crackers," she said.

Mrs. Jenkins went on to list several other songs which the Moral Majority disapproves of:

- "My Favorite Memory" by Merle Haggard. One line recalls "sleeping all night long on the floor." "Probably ate a bunch of crackers before they dozed off," said Mrs. Jenkins.
- "Best Bedroom in Town" by Tammy Wynette. "Doesn't anybody ever get out of bed in Nashville?" asked Mrs. Jenkins.
- "If I Said You Had a Beautiful Body, Would You Hold It Against

Me?" by the Bellamy Brothers. "Utter trash," said Mrs. Jenkins. "I'll bet their mother, Mrs. Bellamy, hides herself in shame every time she hears that song. If Mr. Jenkins had ever said anything like that to me, I would have bashed in his little worm head."

- "My Baby Thinks He's a Train" by Roseanne Cash. "More per version," explained Mrs. Jenkins. "Mr. Jenkins decided he was a Greyhound bus once and that he was leaving."

"What did you do?" I asked her.

"Bashed in his little worm head, of course."

Finally I asked Mrs. Jenkins to name the one song which she feels is most harmful.

"It's by Glen Campbell," she said.

"Glen Campbell?"

"Yes, I know it's hard to believe, but he sings a song called, 'I Love My Truck.' Can you imagine a nice boy from Arkansas getting involved in something like that?"

No, ma'am, I sure can't.


Gospel music, thank the Lord and Mrs. Jenkins, is still safe from such perversion, and I listen to it with gusto and a clean conscience. I get my interest in gospel music honestly. My late father could hunker down on a piano and make it sing a joyful noise as long as there was somebody around to listen.

My Uncle Dorsey on my mother's side rarely missed an all-night gospel sing at the old Atlanta Municipal Auditorium. He favored the bass singer, the tall fellow in the back who always let go on the "Wellawella's," as in, "Wellawella, evuhbody's gon' have a livin' in glowry...."

I grew up in my maternal grandmother's house, and each Sunday morning I awakened to her radio blaring out the "Gospel Jubilee." My grandmother preferred the inevitable short, baby-faced tenor in the quartet who could pop up there higher than a kite with a nearly operatic, "He's my Jeeeeesus!"

Recently I attended the National Gospel Quartet Convention in Nashville, Tennessee, and it was a glooorious event. The auditorium was encircled by those rolling motels that once were Greyhound buses, carrying groups from date to date. On the sides were the names of the groups—the Singing Echoes, the Kingsmen, this family and that.

The auditorium was maybe half full when I entered, but before the night was over it was bulging. In the hallways were booths where gospel fans could buy tapes and albums and autographed photos of their favorite performers. As each quartet left the stage, a spokesperson was given the opportunity to plug the group's wares:

"We're right over yonder at booth fifteen," a man shouted into the microphone, "and we got a three-album-for-fifteen-dollar sale on. Y'all drop by to see us."

There was passion in the music. It jumped and even rocked a bit, and it set toes to tapping and occasionally brought the audience to its feet, heads held toward the heavens, hands clapping.

"We ain't the stars of the show," a fellow said. "Jesus is the star. Let's all stand and give Him a hand!"

Another group walked on, and the lead singer said, "I seen on the marquee out front that the Talking Heads are coming to this auditorium. There's going to be dope-smokin', pill-poppin' and rock music. But you ain't gonna get none of that here tonight. All you gonna get high on is Jeeeesus!"

The crowd loved it.

The last group appeared on the stage and sang its hit song, "Call Me What You Want To, But When He Calls Me, Call Me Gone." The crowd roared following a rousing rendition.

"Sort of gives you glowry bumps listenin' to 'em, don't it?" said the woman sitting next to me.

It does that. It sure does.

# •Are You Nonessential, Undesirable, Unmentionable, or Just Undone?

"In today's automatic car washes, I feel like I'm trapped inside a giant washing machine like a pair of soiled pajamas about to be rinsed to death. If the inside gets cleaned, it's only because my windows leak and the jet sprays soak the interior."

Sometimes you don't have to go out of your way to find opportunities to develop true grit. They'll come to you. Just surviving the lunacy and frustrations of the modern world is evidence of some degree of character. Isn't that why our society always makes such a big deal out of golden wedding anniversaries?

In my particular situation, I travel a lot. Thirty years ago that would have meant many pleasurable train rides with good food, good drink, and plenty of time to read or relax. Today, however, it means airports and airplanes and endless delays and migraine headaches. It starts before you even leave home.

"Good morning, Wingandaprayer Airlines. May I help you?"

"Yes," I said to the voice on the phone. "I'd like to make two round-trip reservations for the Sunday evening flight to Pittsburgh, please."

"Will this be first class, tourist or Wingandaprayer's new cargo class?" she asked.

"Cargo class?"

"Certainly, sir. In an effort to attract your business in these competitive times, Wingandaprayer Airlines is offering an innovative and inexpensive way for you to travel by air. Cargo class simply means you ride in the cargo hold with the baggage at a huge savings in cost. This is available, however, only to those passengers who will fit into their own hanging bags."

"I'll just take tourist," I said.

"Oxygen or non-oxygen?"

"I don't understand."

"Another Wingandaprayer option in our effort to offer passengers a variety of ways to save money and still not have to take the bus," she explained. "If you prefer to bring your own oxygen tank, then your seat will not be equipped with an automatic oxygen mask release in case of sudden cabin depressurization. If Wingandaprayer doesn't have to provide you with oxygen, it can save money and pass those savings along to its customers in the form of reduced fares."

"But I don't have my own oxygen tank."

"In that case, sir, how long can you hold your breath?"

"I'll just take two seats with oxygen."

"Will you be traveling with your wife or another adult?"

"No, I'll be traveling with my nephew Robert, who's six."

"Does he chew Rootie-Tootie Bubble Gum?"

"Is that the kind that turns his teeth blue?" I asked.

"Exactly, sir, and Wingandaprayer now offers free tickets to children if they show eight Rootie-Tootie Bubble Gum wrappers when they go to the agent for their boarding passes. Get 'em while they're young and they're yours forever,' is what we always say at Wingandaprayer," she explained.

"So what is the adult fare?"

"Depends, sir. Will you be cashing in coupons on this trip?"

"Coupons?"

"Check your local newspaper for Wingandaprayer cost-cutting coupons. Bring the coupons with you to the ticket agent and trade them in for savings on your fare."

"OK. Now, will dinner be served on the evening flight to Pittsburgh?"

"Not in tourist, sir. Wingandaprayer lost millions last year, and in an effort to keep our own costs down, we've cut our all meal service except in first class, where passengers are allowed to bob for apples."

"I'll pack a sandwich for me and Robert. Now, will you please see if there is space available on the evening flight to Pittsburgh?"

"I have you confirmed on our 7:20 flight to Pittsburgh, sir. May I have your home address?"

"Why do you need my home address?" I asked.

"So Wingandaprayer can mail you your green stamps and toaster."

When we finally arrived at the airport and boarded the plane, we were immediately greeted by two delays. The first, said the captain, was due to "a minor mechanical problem. We should have it cleared up soon." If an airplane is going to develop a mechanical problem, whether major or minor, the best time to do so is when it's still on the ground. Nonetheless, it can be extremely unsettling to the passengers.

For example, what does the captain consider "minor"? It could be anything from a wing being loose to the navigator's pen being out of ink. Secondly, how can the captain or the passengers know for sure that the problem has been fixed? It's not exactly like dealing with someone's pickup truck, where the mechanic opens the hood, pulls at a few wires and hoses, and then says, "Try it now." If the truck doesn't start, the mechanic pulls at some different wires and hoses. With an airplane, you don't get a second chance.

I expressed my concern to a passing stewardess.

"Don't worry," she said, "our mechanic knows this plane from front to back."

If he knows so much, I thought to myself, why isn't he in the cockpit flying this sucker instead of underneath it pulling at wires and hoses? I looked out the window and saw a fellow who looked like a mechanic scratching his head with a big wrench. On his breast pocket I could read the name, Bobby Earl. Would you trust your life to a man named Bobby Earl?

Another concern was that we were flying on Sunday. Have you ever tried to find a mechanic to work on your car on Sunday? The only ones I've ever found had just been fired from Brake–O. Bobby Earl worked on the plane for about an hour. Then I heard him yell to the pilot, "Try it now!" Sure enough, it started. I didn't know whether to be happy or sad.

As we backed away from the terminal (Why do they have to call it that?), the chief stewardess announced another delay.

"Due to heavy traffic here at the airport, we are presently 108th in line for takeoff, which means we're going to spend approximately four hours and ten minutes either taxiing slowly or sitting in line with a bunch of other planes waiting to take off," she explained.

"Wingandaprayer Airlines would like to apologize for this inconvenience. We realize that some of you have connections or important meetings in Pittsburgh and that this sort of delay could cause you to lose your company's biggest account, among other disastrous occurrences. But please do not whine, because we can't help it if thirty-five other airlines decided to schedule takeoffs at the same time we did.

"We will do everything in our power to make up for this excruciating experience. For those of you who might want to read while we are taxiing out, ask your flight attendant to bring you something from Wingandaprayer's in-flight library. Available today are *War and Peace*, *The Rise and Fall of the Third Reich*, and *The Complete Works of Victor Hugo*.

"Later in our taxi out, we will be offering at no charge our 'Movie While You Wait.' Our feature in first class will be the original, uncut version of *Gone with the Wind*, while our coach passengers will enjoy viewing *Rocky I*, *II*, and *III*.

"If we still haven't taken off by that time, Wingandaprayer has other means of killing time for our passengers. There will be a bridge tournament in rows twenty-five through thirty. For those who prefer bingo, cards may be purchased at a nominal charge. First Officer Willard Smith, who is just as bored as the rest of you, will be calling the games in rows seven through twenty-four.

"In first class there will be Trivial Pursuit games and mud wrestling for any passengers who are interested, as well as a musical performance by two of our flight attendants, Ramona Dentz and Glenda Jane Chastain, singing songs they actually wrote, such as, 'I've Got the Air Sickness Bag Blues.' Other pre-takeoff performances include a lecture by Captain Allis Chalmers, who will explain how to hot-wire a 747, and a demonstration on in-flight macramé by navigator Marco Polonski.

"Also, because of our long delay, our smoking passengers may wish to step outside to smoke. If so, please remember to walk along with the aircraft in case it moves so you don't get too far behind. Thank you for ridin'—, I mean flying, Wingandaprayer Airlines, and have a pleasant flight."

If dealing with airlines doesn't test your mettle and cultivate a little true grit, then try buying or selling a house. Real estate agents are God's curse on mankind when locusts are out of season.

When you're trying to buy a house, there are basically three parties involved: (1) a large lending agency which employs no people, only computers, (2) a real estate agent, who is one of seventeen zillion housewives who got bored with Tuesday morning doubles and went out and got licensed to sell houses, and (3) a working stiff with a wife and two kids.

Here's how the game is played:

The stiff and his wife and two kids have outgrown their modest, 2BR, 1BA, brk. rch. w/o fpl. They are looking for something a little nicer and with more space. They contact a real estate agent, an attractive person named Delores who smokes a lot and drives a late-model Mercedes.

Delores takes the stiff and his wife and his two kids to look at houses that are for sale. The stiff is shown a house with three bedrooms, two baths and a fireplace in the den, which is exactly what he had in mind. Last year it cost seventeen thousand dollars. But that was last year.

"This honey of a place is one-five," says Delores. "One-five" is real estate saleslady talk for one hundred and five big ones. I'm talking thousands.

The poor stiff, meanwhile, is holding about half the down payment and facing an interest rate that would make Shylock cringe.

"But, Darling," says his wife, "it's just perfect, and Marvin and Arnold (the two kids) can each have their own bedroom."

"Yeah, Dad," echo Marvin and Arnold.

This is where the real estate game gets interesting. There's no way the stiff can do what his father probably did—plunk down ten percent and make reasonable payments the rest of his life—so he has to engage in what is termed "creative financing." That's real estate saleslady talk for, "No way can you afford this house, turkey, but I haven't had a good commission in a month, so here's the way we're going to rig it."

There are all sorts of ways to finance a house creatively. Here are a few:

- LOAN ASSUMPTION—That's where you assume your brother-in-law, the doctor, will lend you the money for a down payment, but he laughs in your face and asks if Marvin and Arnold can come over to help him clean his pool.
- WRAPAROUND MORTGAGE—That's where a bunch of fast-talking guys with cigars wrap you around their little fingers and you're in so deep you have to take a night job and Marvin and Arnold forget you exist.
- GRADUATED PAYMENTS—The first year you pay ten dollars a month. The next year you pay ten thousand dollars a month. The following year you live in a tent.
- STARVATION MORTGAGE PLAN—You can make your house payments, but you can't afford food for the first two years of the loan. Marvin and Arnold go to live with your brother-in-law.
- BLACKMAIL—You find out the owner of the house you are trying to buy had a sex-change operation in 1963. "He" gives you the house for free and buys Marvin and Arnold a dog.
- ROB-A-LIQUOR-STORE PLAN—Just what the name implies. You rob liquor stores until you can afford the house. The real es-

tate firm locates the stores and furnishes a stocking to go over your head. Marvin and Arnold watch the doors. Delores drives the getaway car.

Selling a house can be equally frustrating. First the house sits for six months without a single person coming to look at it, but Delores is still nauseatingly optimistic.

"This house will sell. I guarantee it." she says, jingling the change in her pocket and rocking back and forth on her heels.

"Yeah, but during my lifetime?" asks the stiff.

"Trust me," says Delores, popping her gum. Didn't I buy a Pinto from her several years ago? Or was she the travel agent who sold me the Braniff charter to West Beirut?

Finally one afternoon the phone rings and Delores says, "Will it be OK to show the house later today?" What that really means is, "I'll be there in four minutes. These turkeys (prospective buyers) could be hot."

Delores's timing is magnificent. The United States Army Mule Team and its drivers were over for lunch and have just left, and she wants to show the house in four minutes.

"It'll just take me a week to hose the place down," you argue.

"Trust me," says Delores. The Pinto was lemon yellow and the engine sounded like it had emphysema.

The stiff immediately starts throwing things under chairs, under the sofa, into cabinets, and his wife puts something on the stove to boil. That's another tip from Delores: boil cinnamon to give the house a "homey" smell.

"What's that god-awful smell?" asks the man as soon as he walks through the front door.

"Smells like cinnamon to me," says his wife.

"I can't stand the smell of cinnamon. Let's go back and take another look at that house that smelled like garlic. You know, I just love garlic."

Another trick Delores suggests is to have a fire burning in the fireplace. Gives the house a "cozy" feeling, she says.

Only problem is that stiff forgets to open the flue.

"Stay close to the floor and there's plenty of air," says Delores to the prospective buyers. "Now, in there is the master bedroom..."

"Let's get out of here," the man says to his wife. "I'll call the fire department at the first pay phone we see."

I once had a house that sat for nine months without selling. Without so much as thinking about selling. So I did what any self-respecting syndicated columnist would do: I wrote a column about an eccentric old bird who lived there before me and buried two hundred thousand dollars in cash somewhere on the property just before he died. With my bad back, I couldn't even lift a shovel, I wrote, but. . .

In the words of Delores, "Trust me."

Unfortunately, these sorts of shenanigans are not limited to the real estate industry. Deception and misrepresentation are more prevalent today than Boy George. Our very language is twisted and distorted daily so that it's hard to know exactly what phrases mean anymore. Take politics, for example.

When a politician says, "We're still checking the results of our latest poll," what he really means is, "I paid a fortune-teller fifty bucks to predict my chances and she said that if I got two thousand votes she'd eat her crystal ball."

Here are some of their other favorites:

- "A heavy turnout will help us." If all my cousins bother to vote, I might hit double figures.
- "I think bad weather on election day would definitely benefit my opponent." My support is so weak that I'll lose half my votes if there's more than a ten percent chance of rain.
- "We haven't had any attention from the media." I bought drinks for two television reporters and a newspaper columnist, and all I got in return was stuck with a fifty-dollar tab.
- "I don't know how my opponent could stoop so low as to bring up something like that." You rig just one little million-dollar-construction bid and everybody wants to make a federal case out of it.
- "We've run a clean, honest campaign." I spent $25,000 on private detective fees and couldn't come up with a damn thing on my opponent.
- "No matter what the outcome of the election, we've made a lot of new friends all over the country." Especially the blonde at the bar at the Hyatt in San Francisco.
- "I have nothing to be ashamed of." I gave the blonde a fictitious name.

- "You can't run a campaign as inexpensively as you once could." Votes aren't nearly as cheap as they used to be.
- "I'm just a simple country boy." The closest I ever got to a cow was ordering Steak Diane at the country club.
- "It's too early to make any sort of definitive statement on how the election is going." My campaign manager hasn't returned with the booze yet.
- "I want to thank my wife for all her support during the campaign." She believed the story about the lipstick on my shirt after the campaign in San Francisco.
- "I would like to congratulate my opponent on his victory." All I want is five minutes alone with that sorry SOB.
- "Now that the campaign is over, I'm looking forward to getting my life back to normal." I'm not going to sober up for a week.
- "The people have spoken." If I'd known I had that many enemies, I'd have carried a gun.

Politicians and their aides also are forever coming up with catch words or phrases which I find terribly confusing. For example, not long ago President Reagan sent home a lot of "nonessential" government employees because he was fighting with Congress about getting a budget approved.

After his announcement, I couldn't help wondering, What do all those nonessential government employees do? I suppose they handle all the nonessential work the government has to do. But if thousands of government employees are nonessential, what about me? How do I know if I'm essential to the country or not?

To help myself and other Americans answer this crucial question, I devised a test to find out if you're nonessential or not. Just answer the following questions.

1. Is it absolutely necessary that you stay awake and in an upright position while performing your duties?
2. If you walked into the boss's office and demanded a raise, would he (a) give you the raise? (b) throw you out of his office? (c) mistake you for Killiingsworth from accounting who died last year?
3. If you took a leave of absence and hiked the Appalachian trail for six months and came back to work with a full beard, would

anybody notice that you had been away, or, if you're female, remark how it's not everyday that you see a woman with a full beard?

4. Are you with the Ford Motor Company and presently designing a diesel Edsel?

5. If you called in sick, would the boss hire a temporary to fill in, or would he say, "Killingsworth from accounting can handle things until you get back"?

6. If you said, "But, sir, Killingsworth from accounting died last year," would the boss respond, "Too bad, he was a good man," or, "I know. That's why he'd be perfect for your job"?

7. Are you Woody Allen's weight coach?

8. If one day you didn't come to work but sent your dog instead, what most likely would happen? (a) Nobody would notice the difference; (b) The SPCA would cite you for unnecessarily boring a defenseless animal; (c) Your dog would be promoted because he was overqualified for your job.

Finally, if you had the time to take this test while at work, it's a good bet you're nonessential.

Another category of people frequently referred to by the Reagan administration is "undesirables." You might recall several years ago when a former Secretary of the Interior suggested that The Beach Boys might attract "undesirables" to a Washington concert. The Beach Boys, incidentally, are still going strong; the former Secretary now is a fur trapper on the upper east side of Manhattan.

About that same time officials at the University of Texas opposed a Willie Nelson concert on campus because he might attract "undesirables." Since I am one of Willie's biggest fans and attend his concerts at every opportunity, does that make me an undesirable?

Once again, I devised a test to help me and other confused Americans to discover if we are, in fact, undesirable. Just answer truthfully the following questions.

1. When you hear Willie Nelson sing "Up Against the Wall, You Redneck Mother," does it make you want to (a) beat up a hippie; (b) drink beer from a quart jar; (c) take off your shirt; (d) call your mom?

2. Does The Beach Boys's "Little Surfer Girl" make you want

to (a) take narcotics; (b) quit your job and go live at the beach; (c) insult a policeman; (d) ice down some Pepsi and build a sand castle?

3. If you were to attend a Beach Boys concert, which of the following would you likely wear? (a) half a bikini; (b) T-shirt with an obscene message; (c) it doesn't matter because you're going to take it off as soon as you get good and drunk anyway; (d) Gray Flannel cologne.

4. The last time you saw a Willie Nelson concert, which of the following best describes your behavior? (a) loud and obnoxious; (b) nasty and mean; (c) it took a dozen cops to get you into the paddy wagon; (d) you read the latest issue of the *New Yorker* between numbers.

5. Which of the following do you think would come in most handy at your next Beach Boys concert? (a) a hand grenade; (b) your coke dealer; (c) assorted birth control devices (d) an uncrowded restroom.

6. Which of the following would you be most likely to do after attending a Willie Nelson concert? (a) get tattooed; (b) burn a city; (c) rape and pillage; (d) watch "Nightline."

That's it; you can relax now. If you answered (d) to all of the questions, you most certainly are not an undesirable. If you did not answer any questions with (d), you're invited to a party at my house next Saturday night. Dress is not required.

It seems to me that a lot of old-fashioned jobs have been declared non-essential or else those who worked them have been deemed undesirable. For example, what has happened to movie ushers?

It used to be that you bought your ticket and some popcorn and a nice young man in a uniform would lead you with his flashlight to an available seat. You think that wasn't an essential job? You walk into a dark movie theater these days and there's no telling what can happen. You might sit next to a weirdo who makes sucking noises with his teeth. Or worse, you could sit on top of somebody. I walked into a dark theater the other day and was about to comment on how soft and comfortable the seats were when I realized I was sitting on a fat woman's lap.

"Get off me, you weirdo!" she screamed. I scrambled away and landed in another seat on top of a small child, who pinched me. I finally found an empty seat and made sucking noises with my teeth so that I'd be left alone.

And whatever happened to the old-timey car washes? Who declared them nonessential? Years ago people at a car wash would attack your auto with brushes and rags, and then they'd sweep and vacuum the inside of the car. Not even the Methodist Youth Fellowship car washes do that anymore. It's important to have the inside of your car cleaned occasionally. I did so recently and found two dollars in change, a missing tennis shoe and an old friend I thought had moved to Wyoming.

In today's automatic car washes, I feel like I'm trapped inside a giant washing machine like a pair of soiled pajamas about to be rinsed to death. If the inside gets cleaned, it's only because my windows leak and the jet sprays soak the interior.

And where, pray tell, are the old door-to-door salesmen? Nobody comes to my house selling magazines or encyclopedias or vacuum cleaners anymore.

"Hi," the young man would say. "My name is Harvey and I'm working my way through college and I'm trying to win this contest...."

I don't remember ever buying anything from those salesmen, but at least it kept them off the streets and gave the dogs a little sport that was safer than chasing cars. What could be more essential?

In place of those important old jobs, we now have people doing the most absurd jobs imaginable. Just who are those people in the bathrooms everywhere I go? Do their wives know what they're doing?

I've been able to go to the bathroom without assistance since I was five or six, but lately every time I turn around I'm confronted by a smiling, grown man bearing towels. For the use of one, I'm expected to drop something spendable into his tip dish. I admit that I'm not very mechanically inclined, but I can usually figure out a towel dispenser or even one of those electric blowers without help.

There are, of course, ways to avoid rest room attendants. You can leave quickly without washing your hands, or you can simply hand the towel back to the attendant, smile, and say thank you. If he still wants a tip, tell him to plant his corn early next year.

Not washing your hands can be unsanitary, however, or even unsociable. I was standing at a urinal beside two fellows at a Georgia-

Auburn football game once. The Georgia fan, dressed in red and black from head to toe, finished his business, zipped his pants and headed for the door.

"Hey, Bulldog," shouted the Auburn fan, "don't they teach you guys at Georgia to wash after using the bathroom?"

"No," said the Bulldog fan, "they teach us not to piss on our hands."

I'm a dyed-in-the-wool Bulldog, and that's why I don't need anybody in the bathroom handing me a towel.

Being nonessential, undesirable or even outmoded is minor compared to the shame that can result from being associated with the unmentionables. I'm not referring to disreputable characters, but rather to women's lingerie. Buying it, even for your wife, can be more embarrassing than urinals that splash.

In the first place, you never know who might see you.

"Guess who I saw in Willoughby's buying lingerie," says one busybody to another.

"Who?"

"Harvey Nelson, that's who."

"Never would have figured him for the kinky type."

"I feel sorry for his poor wife and children."

You can't walk into a lingerie department with a big grin on your face and say, "I'm not buying these for myself," because everyone will assume that you certainly are; neither can you walk in announcing, "These are for my wife, you know," because everyone will assume that they certainly are not. In such situations, I recommend a disguise, such as wearing dark glasses and speaking with a foreign accent.

"May I help you, sir?" the saleslady will ask.

"*Sí*," you answer. "I would like to look at your nightgown collection, *por favor.*"

The saleslady will have no idea she is selling good ol' Harvey Nelson something that the Catwoman on Bourbon Street wouldn't wear.

"I'll tell you something, Mildred," she'll say to her friend at lunch. "Those French are everything they say they are."

There are a couple more "don'ts" which I would recommend to any man who finds himself in this situation:

- Don't ask the saleslady to try on lingerie "since you're about the same size as my wife."
- Don't inquire about the possibility of purchasing the especially attractive mannequin in the black nightie. This could lead to an embarrassing arrest.
- Don't buy your wife or mistress colored underpants with the days of the week or the Clemson football schedule printed on them. For some reason, most women don't like them.

One of the greatest personal adversities I must endure, one that develops the patience and grit in me, is the frequent abuse of my last name. A man's name is his birthright, and to have it besmudged is a terrible thing.

Only recently someone sent me an advertisement from the local newspaper in which a grocery store was offering "Fresh Chicken Grizzards" at seventy-nine cents a pound. The loving folks who sent me the ad included a notation: "Know the difference between a gizzard and a grizzard? One's just part of a chicken. The other is the whole thing."

To think that riffraff like that are allowed to use the public mails.

What obviously happened in the ad was that someone made a small error. By inserting an *r* in gizzards (which aren't worth seventy-nine cents a pound, no matter how you spell 'em), they libeled my proud name. It's not the first time, I must admit. People of little breeding often pronounce my name without the *r*. In restaurants they're always blurting out, "Gizzard, party of four. The Gizzard party, please." I save a lot of money on tips when that happens.

Other people simply mispronounce the name by making it rhyme with lizard. It does not. Notice the two *z*'s, which means that Grizzard should be pronounced GrizZARD, which is French in origin and means "wild stallion."

There have been some very famous GrizZARDS down through the years who have made the name synonymous with noble deeds and glory. There was Pierre GrizZARD, a famous French sheetrocker who is given credit for many of the aesthetic qualities of the Palace of Versailles.

Then there was Jean Paul GrizZARD, the French trapper who single-handedly introduced several different strains of venereal disease to the

North American Indians in the middle of the eighteenth century.

And, of course, there was my great-great-great-grandfather, Brigadier General Beauregard GrizZARD of the Confederate Army, who successfully defended Miami Beach against the yankees during the Civil War, something no one else has been able to do since.

Yes, mine is a proud name, steeped in history and tradition. To have it abused in some grocery ad is a personal affront to me and my kin. And for anyone who is thinking about writing me a letter to that insidious joke about Mr. BuzZARD who's in the yard, and Mr. TurTELL who's at the well, and Mr. RabBIT, etc., don't bother. Mr. GrizZARD has already heard it a million times.

Of all the trials and tribulations I face, one of the most difficult certainly is Sunday nights. I hate Sunday nights. I think this hatred goes back to my childhood.

Sunday mornings when I was growing up were wonderful. We got up early with the radio blaring gospel music through the house, ate a wonderful breakfast of homemade biscuits and ham or bacon and then got ready for Sunday school.

I had only one white shirt and wore it every Sunday. My mother would wash it, hang it on the line to dry in the Southern sunshine and then iron it by hand. There is a special place in heaven for women who spent days of their lives ironing.

Sunday school itself was a social event. They put us kids in the basement and for an hour we sang songs like, "Do, lord, oh do, lord, oh do remember me, praise Jesus!" The sermon hour wasn't as easy. I watched the hands on my mother's watch crawl as I drew hills and birds on the title pages of the hymnals. I hope the Great Scorer doesn't hold that against me; I was only nine.

Then came that wonderful Sunday lunch, featuring fried chicken and rice and gravy and plump prizes from the garden. And, of course, more homemade biscuits. My mother always let me fork the first piece of white meat. I hope someday I love a child enough to let them do the same.

On Sunday afternoons my friends and I dammed creeks and watched trains or rode bikes or hit rocks with broom handles. Then as the sun got low in the sky, we'd gather on the front porch and start talking about supper. But it was never an organized meal—just left-over chicken and biscuits whenever you wanted it.

I think that's where my problem with Sunday evenings began. I was a grown man before I stopped pouting that my mother made me get my own supper on Sunday evenings. Inevitably there was no white meat left, only dark. And the only thing on television was Ed Sullivan with seals and jugglers. It was a depressing way to end what had been a wonderful day.

Sunday nights still feel the same way. They depress me. I take a lot of Sunday night meals alone these days, and many times I would be thankful for a cold piece of dark meat. There's still nothing much on TV, just an occasional "60 Minutes" piece on germ warfare that depresses me even more.

There's a distinct quiet on Sunday nights. A lonely quiet. I get sentimental. I call a few old friends, we talk, hang up and the quiet is even quieter. I try to work a lick but my mind won't have it. It's too late to call anyone else. I eat some tuna fish straight from the can.

I also pray on Sunday nights, whether I feel the need to or not. Give Monday a little shove, Lord. Do.

Finally, for those citizens of the world who endure it daily, who confront idiocy and walk away from it a better man or woman for having done so, I offer some questions that don't necessarily match but are worthy of your consideration nonetheless.

THE QUESTIONS:
- Why is it that no matter which lane you're in on the expressway, the other one is always moving faster?
- Who ate the first oyster?
- Who said convenience stores are convenient? As compared to what?
- Why do service stations lock the bathroom door but leave the cash register unlocked?
- Is it really necessary for bowling balls to be that heavy?
- Do animals go to heaven when they die?
- Did Michael Jackson or Boy George ever play any sports?
- What are chicken fingers that so many restaurants are serving these days? I didn't know they had fingers.
- Why is it I have sixty channels on my television and still can't

find anything worth watching?
- What makes popcorn pop?
- What happened to the power in modern automobiles? They're wonderful for funeral processions but no match for a strong headwind.
- Why aren't there any black hockey players?
- What are those little green things in fruitcake?

THE ANSWERS:
- Most of the things your mother told you are true. Disregard the part about eating liver to live longer; it's not worth it.
- Life isn't fair. That's what makes it so interesting.
- Money doesn't grow on trees, and if it did somebody else would own the orchard.
- If you have to shoot it, don't drink it.
- The greatest benefit of going to college is learning to get up in the morning without somebody making you.
- Going to church on Sunday morning will make you feel better no matter what you did on Saturday night.
- The best things in life aren't free. Just ask any poor person.
- Never buy anything from a man who jingles his change.
- If you can't flow, flee.

# •Profiles in Gray Grit

As an only child in a traditional Southern family, I grew up around adults. Not just my parents, but grandparents and uncles and aunts as well. It was an extended family long before anyone decided to call it that. While they sat on the front porch rocking and shelling peas and telling tales, I picked beggar lice off my pants legs and listened closely. That was probably the best education I ever received, and as I look back on it now from the perspective of middle age, I realize there was more wisdom on that porch than I ever imagined. Listen to a few of these stories of senior citizens and you'll see what I mean.

# A Private War on Hunger

My grandmother, Willie Word, declared her own war on hunger years before it became the international issue that it is today. "Every stray dog and cat in the county seems to wind up here," she used to say. It was easy to figure out why. Every stray dog and cat in the county had gotten the word that when all else failed, you always could get a hand-out at Willie Word's house.

My grandmother also made certain that birds around her yard never went hungry, and when my grandfather complained that the worms had gotten into his tomatoes, she would say, "Even worms have to have something to eat, you know."

She fed her family well, too, of course. My favorite from her table was pork chops. Biting through the flaky crust and succulent meat remains my taste buds' unanimous choice as childhood's best culinary memory. I was an admitted glutton when it came to Mama Willie's pork chops. She always cooked two each for every member of the family, but I always managed to get three.

"Want my last pork chop?" she inevitably asked me, and I inevitably accepted.

One afternoon as I was walking home from a friend's house, I spotted an old man, a tramp, I supposed, lying on the front steps of the Baptist church across the street from where we lived. When I got inside, I told Mama Willie about him.

"He's probably hungry," said my grandmother, who promptly went across the street and fetched him.

He was hungry. You could see it in his eyes as he watched Mama Willie prepare dinner, to which she had invited him. A pork chop dinner. I counted heads and pork chops as we prepared to deliver the blessing. There were five people and only eight pork chops. I was immediately concerned about my usual three.

Mama Willie passed out the pork chops. She placed two on my plate, two on my mother's plate and two on my grandfather's plate. Somebody, I reasoned, is going to miss out on a marvelous pork chop dinner if this trend continues. Then my grandmother gave the ragged old man the other two chops, denying herself any meat that night.

Where, I wondered, is my usual third chop coming from? I ate my first one in a hurry. As I started on my second, I noticed my grandmother staring at me. I looked down at the second pork chop. I looked back at Mama Willie. She motioned her head toward the tramp, who had gone through his two chops in record time and was now attacking the bones. I knew what she wanted me to do.

I had to spit out the words. "Would you like my last pork chop?"

"I'd be much obliged," he said.

I looked back at my grandmother. She was smiling at me.

I haven't sent any money to help the starving people in Ethiopia yet, but I think I will. The memory of that smile demands it.

# Honest, Mom, It's No Trouble

It's the same story every year at Christmas.

"Son," says my mother, "you don't have to get me anything for Christmas this year."

And I say, "I know that, Mother, but I want to get you something for Christmas."

"Well, I just don't want to be any trouble."

"It won't be any trouble, Mother. That's part of the enjoyment of Christmas, buying gifts."

"There's just no reason to waste your money on me, son."

"Buying you a Christmas present isn't exactly wasting my money," I argue.

"But there's really nothing I need."

"There must be something you need or want."

"You gave me pajamas last year. I have plenty of pajamas."

"So how about house shoes, the fluffy kind?"

"I have a closet full of house shoes already," she says.

"How about a nice nightgown?"

"I'll never use all the nightgowns I have now. Why don't you just take the money you would have spent on me and buy yourself something nice? Do you have a warm coat?"

"Yes, Mother. Three of 'em."

"How about sweaters?"

"I could start my own line of sweaters, I have so many."

"How about a hat?"

"I don't wear hats."

"Well, how do you keep your head warm?"

"My head doesn't get cold."

"You need a hat in the winter. You might catch a cold if you don't wear a hat."

"This is ridiculous. We're supposed to be talking about what I'm going to get you for Christmas."

"What could you get me? I never go anywhere anymore."

"How about a Jacuzzi?"

"A what?"

"You'd love it. A Jacuzzi is a tub that you fill with hot water, and there are all these jets shooting out water. You sit in there and it's very relaxing. It would be great for your arthritis."

"I never heard of such a thing," she parries.

"What we could do is knock out a wall and extend the bathroom and put the Jacuzzi there."

"I don't want a bunch of carpenters sawing and hammering and tracking mud into the house. Don't get me a bacuzzi."

"Jacuzzi."

"However you say it, I don't want it."

"I know there must be something you'd like to have for Christmas," I persist.

"OK. What I really would like is a pantsuit to wear when I go to the doctor."

"Great. Why didn't you say that in the first place?"

"I didn't want to be a bother."

"It's no bother. What size?"

"Sixteen. Don't let 'em sell you a fourteen, because that's too small."

"What color?"

"Any color, except red."

"Why not red?"

"I'm too old to wear red."

"OK, one non-red pantsuit. Anything else?"

"That's plenty, son. I don't want to be a bother to you."

The pantsuit I bought my mother is blue. It was no bother whatsoever.

# • The Bigger They Are, The More They Weigh

Not everybody gets out of life what they put into it. Some folks work hard all their days and never free themselves from the bog of poverty. Others just bounce through life like a pinball, taking the easiest path but lighting up things and racking up points all the way. Yet from one end of the tax scale to the other, from *Who's Who* to the welfare rolls, real character looks the same.

# A Story of Courage and Dignity

She said she remembered the first time she ever saw him. "I was in seventh-grade music class in my hometown of Provo, Utah," she began. "The teacher introduced us to a new boy who had just moved into town from New York. He was wearing knickers. He had on a pullover sweater and a little cap. He wore them every day. I found out later he was so poor that's all his mother could afford."

They became friends. They moved on to high school together, and they attended dances together.

"He told me there were two reasons he took me to dances," she recalled. "He said he liked me, of course, but I also had paid for my activities card, so he didn't have to pay a nickel to get me in."

Una Clark is a bright, pert lady with an easy smile. She lives in Seattle, Washington. Does her name sound familiar? That's right, Mrs. Barney Clark, widow of the first human recipient of an artificial heart. Dr. Barney Clark, the little boy in knickers, grew up to be a dentist. He developed heart problems, and when there was no alternative, he agreed to try the artificial heart. It kept him alive 112 days.

"We did hope there would be personal gain if we agreed to the artificial heart," said Mrs. Clark, "but Barney also felt this was something he could do for his fellow man. Somebody had to be first."

I wanted to know more about Una and Barney Clark's life together. After Dr. Clark died, his doctor said one of the reasons he was able to live as long as he did was because of the strong support he had from his family, because he had a wife who loved him dearly. I wanted to know how such a relationship came about.

"Barney never had much confidence," Mrs. Clark said. "He never told me how he felt about me. His father had died when he was very young, and he had been so insecure, so poor. I think that's what caused his lack of confidence. Maybe if he had said he cared about me, something would have happened when we were younger, but I never had any idea he wanted anything serious between us. I married his best friend."

That was just before the outbreak of World War II. Una Clark's husband was a flier. He died in action.

"Barney called me when he heard what had happened," she said. "It wasn't long after that when we found out we loved each other."

Dr. Barney Clark was a bombardier during the war. It was his service record, said his wife, that gave him the confidence he had never had before. He went to dental school after the war and established a successful practice.

"Everything he did, he went after it hard." said Una Clark. "If there was anything about him I could criticize, it would be that he was selfish with his time. He was a workaholic. If I could have changed him, I would have made him spend more time with me."

The man showed awesome courage in agreeing to become the first artificial heart recipient. His last days were spent in the discomfort of tubes and tests. But as his wife said, somebody had to be first. As one who has benefited directly from heart research, Una and Barney Clark are heroes to me.

One more thing I had to ask. "Do you miss him?"

"Yes," she answered softly. "I miss him very much."

We all do.

# Forgive Him and Toast His Memory

Marvin Griffin was governor of the State of Georgia from 1955-59. When he died in 1982, most of his eulogies included an apology for the fact that he once stood tall for segregation.

Running for political office has a lot in common with show business. You give the people what they want. When Marvin Griffin ran for governor, what the people of Georgia wanted—at least those who could vote—was a segregationist. If you felt differently in those days, about the only thing you could run for was the state line.

I'm not launching a defense of Marvin Griffin's politics; I'm just pointing out that he wasn't singing a solo.

As a person, I liked him very much. I first met him a dozen years ago in a bar. I introduced myself and told him my grandfather had been one of his most ardent admirers.

"What is yo' granddaddy's name, son?" he asked me.

I told him.

"Yes, indeed," said the former governor. "A fine man. I know him well. And how is his health?"

"Been dead for ten years," I answered.

"Sorry to hear that, son," said Uncle Marvin. "Let's toast his memory."

Some are born to politick, and I've never drunk with a better practitioner of the art. He had a million great lines, and he growled them in a classic Southernese. He was a big man, robust and full of life. When he talked, he played with each word, milking it for all it was worth.

He was asked once, after his term as governor was over, if he had any advice for young politicians. "Tell 'em to remember just two things," he said. "Keep yo' mouth shut and yo' bowels open."

The last time I saw him was at a banquet before a big Georgia football game. He was the opening speaker and forgot at least the first part of his advice to young politicians. The thousands assembled nearly missed the kickoff of the football game, but I loved every minute of it. There'll be other games, but only one Marvin Griffin.

"Man came up to me one time when I was campaigning in the Fayette County," he reminisced, " and said, 'Governor, let's me and you go have a little drink.' I said, 'My friend, soon as I see to it that everybody in Fayette County knows my name, I'll go drink a mule's earful with you.'"

Forgive him his opportunistic bellowings for segregation. Forgive him the improprieties of his administration. He added color to our lives and made us some memories, he did. A mule's earful.

# • From Sea to Shining Sea

"In Florence, my traditional American values were challenged on every corner. You see, there are a million statures in Florence, and every one of them is naked... Try as I may, I just can't picture Stonewall Jackson on his horse in the town square wearing nothing but his sword. It ain't fittin'."

As I've tried to demonstrate, true grit is not indigenous to any group or any place. Some of the best examples of the developing and the finished product I've seen, for instance, appeared in Italy.

I was there for three weeks of R&R (Note to IRS agents: That stands for Research and Reflection. I worked night and day, as this chapter proves, and that's why I was forced to list the trip as a deduction). Like most tourists, the first challenge I had to face was the language. To better prepare myself, I bought one of those Berlitz guides of "two thousand helpful phrases."

They were right. The guide would have been very helpful...if I had been having a convulsion. The way to say, "I am having a convulsion," in Italian is "*Io ho le convulsioni.*" But who's got time to look it up if they're having a convulsion face down in pasta? If they really wanted to be helpful in those books, they would tell you how to say, "Last night I went out and got drunker than a four-eyed Italian dog, and I desperately need something for this hangover." I couldn't find that phrase anywhere. And I needed it. Bad.

The book did provide me with a useful phrase for the train. The way to say, "I think you are in my seat." is "*Penso che questo sia il mio posto.*" What it didn't do, however, was tell me what to say when the fellow in my seat was the toughest hombre in Genoa, and he replied with an Italian phrase which I interpreted to mean, "One more word out of you, salami-face, and I'll slice you up like so much prosciutto."

What I finally did was what most Americans do when they can't speak the language. I started using American-Italian, which means putting a vowel on the end of each English word and waving your arms a lot. For instance, if you want to say, "You are standing on my foot," in Italian, you say, "*Youo areo standingo ona mya footta.*" If you look down and point at your foot, it will helpo.

Italians, to their credit, will attempt to speak English with you, thus making it easier for visitors in their country. There is a problem here, too, however: Italians, especially taxi drivers and waiters, know only certain English phrases, and they use them for a multitude of responses.

"If you don't slow down," you might say to the taxi driver, "you are going to kill us all!"

To which he will reply, "Dank you berry much."

Or, to your waiter you say, "This soup is rancid."

"Meddy Chreestmas," he replies.

All the communications problems I had in Italy reminded me of a similar problem Bogator Green, the world famous mechanic from my hometown, once had. An Italian couple was driving through in a rental car when it developed engine trouble. A local deputy sheriff came to their rescue and had the car towed to Bogator's "garage," a large shade tree behind his trailer.

The couple spoke no English, and Bogator was only slightly better versed in Italian. After checking their car, Bogator said, "Your manifold's busted."

The man shook his head in bewilderment.

"He's Italian, Bogator," said the deputy sheriff. "He doesn't understand you."

"Oh," said Bogator. He then cupped his hands around his mouth and screamed in the man's ear, "YOUR MANIFOLD'S BUSTED!"

Once you've mastered the language, another way Americans build character in Italy is by walking the streets.

"You go out for a walk?" asked the bellman at my hotel in Rome.

"Yes," I replied.

"Be careful," he suggested. "The drivers are very aggressive here." And the Pope is Catholic, he might have added.

In a matter of minutes, I had figured it out—it was a game of demolitionio derbyo. The buses try to run over the cars. The cars try to run over what seems to be everybody and his Italian brother on a motor scooter. And all three try to run down the helpless pedestrians, who are nothing more than human bowling pins. The taxi driver who drove me from the train station to my hotel narrowly missed picking up a 7–10 split on the Via Condetti, and he left an easy spare on the Via Veneto when a shopper dived away from his speeding taxi just in time.

"An Italian taxi driver," said another man at the hotel, "would try to run over his grandmother if she got in his way." I guess that explains the shortage of Italian grandmothers I noted in Rome. I finally figured out that red lights are merely for decoration in Italy, brakes routinely last one hundred thousand miles since they're seldom used, and the quickest way to become rich is to open a body and paint shop.

"Why do people drive this way in Rome?" I asked the bellman.

"Because," he laughed, "ninety-five percent of the Italian people think they are Beppe Gabbiana."

"Beppe Gabbiani?" I asked.

"Richard Petty, to you."

That cleared it up nicely.

In Florence, my traditional American values were challenged on every corner. You see, there are a million statues in Florence, and every one of them is naked.

There's "David" by Michelangelo, a masterpiece completed in 1504 when the artist was only twenty-five years old. David makes Bo Derek look overdressed.

There's "The Rape of the Sabine Women" by Giambologna. Children under seventeen must be accompanied by a parent or legal guardian to get a gander at this one.

"Hercules and Diomedes" by Vicenzo de Rossi apparently is a tribute to the sport of wrestling. If you liked watching Argentina Rocca throw Lou Thesz out of the ring, you'll adore "Hercules and Diomedes."

"Perseus" by Cellini is another example of a woman losing her head over a man, and "Bacchus's Fountain" is a sculpture of a fat man riding a turtle. Must be some sort of tribute to Italian turtle racing.

We are not accustomed to such rampant nudity in the United States, and any time it appears, there is always some group stepping forward to protect us. I remember when Marvin Knowles, a fellow from my hometown, made it big in professional wrestling. Using the name "The Masked Pork Chop," Marvin wrestled in National Guard armories and high school gymnasiums as far away as Tupelo, Mississippi.

Because of the acclaim he brought to our town, the local ladies club arranged for "Marvin Knowles Day," which would feature the unveiling of a statue of Marvin in his ring crouch, to be placed on the elementary school ballfield where Marvin got his start wrestling Cordie Mae Poovey, the ugliest and meanest girl in town. The day before the unveiling, however, some of the ladies dropped by to inspect the statue and were shocked to find Marvin wearing nothing but his wrestling tights. They had the sculptor back the next morning before dawn, carving Marvin a pair of loose-fitting underdrawers that reached all the way down to his wrestling boots.

I think maybe they were right. Try as I may, I just can't picture Stonewall Jackson on his horse in the town square wearing nothing but his sword. It ain't fittin'.

By the time I reached Venice, I was delighted to hear Americans talking at a table beside me during dinner. It was an elderly couple grappling with noodles and salmon and drinking white wine from a pitcher. I asked where they were from.

"Massachusetts," said the lady, obviously someone's grandmother.

"Originally from Arizona, though," her husband added. He had the look of an ex-soldier.

Apparently they also were glad to hear a voice from home, and we swapped stories over dinner that night. They were both widowed, the lady said, but had been friends back in Arizona before their mates had died. Living alone had not appealed to either of them, so they had married recently. Their eyes met and stayed together as she talked about their marriage.

"So this is a honeymoon?" I asked.

"Just a nice, long trip," the man said. I think I noticed a blush as he spoke. He had started slowly in the conversation, but now the wine was beginning to take effect. They were to be in Europe for three months, he said. First they had visited Germany, then it was on to Austria. The old man told me about the archbishop who once ruled over Salzburg.

"He built a large house," he explained. "And why would an archbishop need such a large house? For the women he kept there who gave him fifteen illegitimate sons!"

The old man roared with laughter. There's at least a spark left there, I thought.

"Newspaperman," I answered when they asked. The old man brightened again. What a coincidence, he said; his brother-in-law used to be a newspaperman, too.

"He was the music critic for the Washington Post, the one Harry Truman threatened to kick where you don't want to be kicked when he questioned Margaret Truman's musical talents. Years later, my brother-in-law was visiting Independence, Missouri, and was going through the Truman library. Somebody recognized him and asked if he would like to say hello to the former President. Well, of course he would, and do you know what Truman said to him?"

No, I couldn't imagine.

"He said my brother-in-law was right all along. He said his daughter Margaret really didn't have much talent as a musician." The man roared again with laughter.

It was getting late. The man started into the story about the archbishop again.

"You've already told that one, dear," his wife said.

I offered my good-byes and said maybe we would see each other again sometime. Of course, we wouldn't, but Americans always tell each other that sort of thing. As I left, I heard the man ask his wife, "One more half-liter of wine before bed?"

"OK, let's have one more half-liter," she answered, smiling at him.

Oh, to be young—relatively or otherwise—and in love as night falls on Venice. Or even Cleveland.


I can't think of anything, short of gun-totin' federal marshals, that would make me move out of the United States. But if for any reason I ever had to pick another country to live in, I think it would be Switzerland.

In the first place, it's a naturally beautiful country with mountain peaks and crystal clear lakes. It's also very clean, the banks are discreet, it's a nice place to shop for cheese and watches, and the taxi service is wonderful.

Most of the cabs in Switzerland are late model Mercedeses or BMWs. I've ridden in taxis in the U.S. that were so old the driver had to pull off the road and re-shoe his mule. Also, when a taxi picks you up in Switzerland, the driver gets out and opens the door for you. In the U.S., most taxi drivers are surlier than Mr. T with a bad case of hemorrhoids and wouldn't open the door for their grandmother if she were carrying a steamer trunk.

Here are some other nice things about Switzerland:

- When you cross the street, motorists stop and allow you to pass. In most American cities, it's open season on pedestrians.
- When you swim in a Swiss pool, you must wear a bathing cap. I asked the pool attendant why. "You shouldn't have to swim

with other people's hair floating in the water," she said. Darn straight.

- There are very few billboards along the Swiss roadways. You can actually see the countryside.
- While I was in Switzerland, I didn't see a single snake or mosquito.
- The air in Switzerland doesn't burn your nose, and when the temperature reaches eighty, they think they're having a heat wave.
- I don't think they have much of a crime problem in Switzerland, either. I base this assumption on an experience I had in Lugano.

    I noticed a man down on his hands and knees drawing a beautiful picture of the Virgin Mary on the sidewalk with colored chalk. Around the man were several shoe boxes in which those who appreciated his artwork had dropped coins. The following evening I happened to pass by the same spot. The artist was gone, but the shoe boxes were still there along with the day's collection. "You mean to say," I asked a native, "that he can leave his coins out there all night and nobody will steal them?" The man looked shocked. "Steal from a poor artist?" he asked. "Who would steal from the poor?"

    That's another thing I like about Switzerland: It still has a ways to go to catch up with the rest of civilization.

Of course, if Italy or even Switzerland isn't your cup of wine, there are many other options for interesting vacations closer to home which can also teach you about the world and the wonderful characters who populate it. Here are just a few American vacation packages I could recommend:

- GALA ARKANSAS—Four days and five nights in the "Land of the Razorback." Learn to stand on a table in a restaurant and scream, "Sooooooooie Piiiig!" like the happy University of Arkansas football fans do when they go out of town. Learn to jump-start a pickup truck like the University of Arkansas foot ball fans do when they try to get back home. Visit the lovely Ozarks and stay in a real mountain shack near Dogpatch, USA. See first hand what outdoor plumbing is all about! The kids will love it! (Soap, towels, heat, lights, snakebite kits, and ammunition NOT included.)

- THE OTHER FLORIDA—Tired of crowded beaches and fancy hotels? Then this might be just right for you. A trip off Florida's beaten paths to lovely, exciting Bugspray Swamp Resort, located in the mysterious Everglades. Explore the hidden world of reptiles and insects with guide, cook and medicine man. Take a hike in Quicksand Alley. (Who got left behind?) See mosquitoes the size of eagles and gnats as big as bats. Four days, five nights, and six chances out of ten that at least one member of your family gets eaten by an alligator.

- OLD SOUTH TOUR—Get a real feel for the Old South with a tour of Fort Deposit, Alabama, and meet Fort Deposit's leading citizen, Billy Bob Bailey, and his dog, Rooster. See the local diner where Governor George Wallace once had lunch during a campaign trip. See the local hospital where the governor recuperated. Visitors from New Jersey and other places Up North will want to ask Billy Bob about his special deals on souvenirs, like water actually carried by soldiers during the Civil War, dirt from historic Civil War battlefields and trained boll weevils. And, if you're lucky, Rooster might even do some tricks for northern friends, like removing their distributor caps. Don't worry. Billy Bob's Service Station, located next to the souvenir shop, is open twenty-four hours a day.

- NUDE BEACH—Just think of it! Nude swimming, nude tennis, nude golf, and nude volleyball. And we know just the rock you can hide behind to see it all. Film extra.

- DINOSAUR WORLD—Located off Highway 78 near beautiful downtown Snellville, Georgia. Huge replicas of dinosaurs and other prehistoric animals. Great fun for the kids and educational, too. Would you like to own Dinosaur World yourself? Ask for Harvey and make him an offer. Any offer.

- DUDE RANCH—Here's a dude ranch with a new twist. Instead of riding a bunch of smelly horses, ride dinosaurs and other prehistoric animals. Located off Highway 78 near beautiful downtown Snellville, Georgia. Tell Harvey, the dude who got stuck with this joint, to "saddle 'em up!"

If your tastes run more to the great outdoors, I could recommend a rafting trip down the raging Colorado River. But before you sign up for

such an arduous undertaking, you may want to ask a few questions—
to which I already have the answers.

1.  How do I get to the Colorado River? Fly from Las Vegas out
    into the middle of the Arizona desert in a small airplane (envi-
    sion a '53 Ford with wings) and land in a wide place be-
    tween two cacti. Then ride a mule down the treacherous
    ledges of the canyon to the river and pray the mule doesn't
    make one alse step, because mules, unfortunately, don't have
    wings.

2.  How can the Arizona desert best be described? Ten zillion acres
    of dust.

3.  Is there ever a change of scenery? Occasionally you see a
    cow pie.

4.  Once on the river, are the rapids exciting? Lie down on a
    waterbed and get a small child to jump up and down on it.
    Same thing, except you don't get as wet.

5.  How hot is it on the river? During the day, about 120 degrees,
    but at night it cools down nicely to maybe 102.

6.  Where do you camp? On sandy river banks.

7.  What is it like camping when the wind starts blowing at night?
    Think of a blast furnace.

8.  What do you eat on the trip? Mostly sand.

9.  How did the brochure describe camping at night along the
    river? "…Drift slowly off to sleep under the starry western
    skies as you are caressed by a cool breeze, the restful sound of
    rushing water, and the pleasant blend of guitars and mellow
    voices."

10. Has the person who wrote the brochure ever actually taken
    the trip? No.

11. Was there anybody interesting along with you? Yes. A newly-
    wed couple on their honeymoon.

12. What do you call people who take a rafting trip down the
    raging Colorado for their honeymoon? Weird.

13. Did you encounter any scorpions? Yes, but the red ants were
    worse. Scorpions sting only in self-defense; red ants bite be-
    cause they enjoy it.

14. What about rattlesnakes? Don't worry. We never found more
    than one at a time in a sleeping bag.

15. What are the restroom facilities like in camp? A little green tent.
16. What is the most important thing to know about camping on the Colorado River? Never spread your bedroll near the little green tent.
17. Will you ever take such a trip again? Sure, as soon as mules sprouts wings and fly.

I used to recommend Hilton Head, South Carolina, as a wonderful getaway, but not long ago a friend sent me a clipping from the island's newspaper which warned of trouble. For the sake of an informed public, following is a reprint of that article:

Members of an elite corps of South Carolina state militia stormed the beach here Saturday and reclaimed the plush resort from thousands of Northern vacationers who took over the island several years ago after surrendering Miami Beach.

"Hilton Head is a part of the sovereign state of South Carolina," declared Governor Willis Peabody, "and nobody else has any right to any part of the soil our forefathers grabbed off the Indians. Any attempt to retake the island will result in the gravest of consequences."

The governor would not elaborate on what he meant by "gravest of consequences," but the South Carolina militiamen have put the island under what some of the Northern vacationers are referring to as "the next thing to martial law." One new order disallows the sale of piña colada mix to anyone who cannot prove he or she was born south of Richmond, Virginia.

Hilton Head Island, with miles of beach, numerous golf courses and tennis courts and Ralph Lauren's coastal headquarters, is just off the South Carolina mainland near the Georgia port city of Savannah.

The pre-brunch raid which reclaimed the island was believed to have been launched from Williams' Seafood Restaurant in Savannah in bass boats rented from the Thunderbolt Marina, Bait, and Tackle. "We even brought our own beer," said Captain Charlie "Swamp Fox" Ravenel, head of the Carolina militia.

It is believed that the militia also included volunteers from the neighboring state of Georgia, which has had a recent problem with a growing number of Northerners moving into its Golden Isles resorts of Jekyll Island, St. Simons Island, and Sea Island. This belief was stimulated by reports that some of the militiamen, upon storming across the beach and reaching the lobby of the Hilton Head Inn, cried out, "How 'bout them Dawgs!"—a familiar Georgia exclamation for any occasion, including selected funerals.

The Northern occupants of the island, including visitors from the Canadian province of Ontario who were on the island looking for reptile farms and glass-bottom boats, were caught completely off guard by the attack. There apparently was only one casualty, however; a lady from Akron, Ohio, on the beach to catch some early rays, was stepped on by an attacking militiaman and suffered a pair of broken sunglasses.

"You can spot yankee men on the beach from a mile out in the ocean," Captain Ravenel said. "They all wear Bermuda shorts, sandals, and black socks pulled up to their armpits. But yankee women, they put on those white bathing suits and they haven't been in the sun in so long, then blend right into the sand. My man said he thought that lady was some kind of jellyfish that had washed up on the beach. If he'd have looked a little closer, he'd have seen her mustache and probably would have missed her."

Reaction came swiftly from the North. One possible retaliatory move, said Governor Fitzhugh Stratsworth III of Ohio, was to move the Ohio National Guard south of Hilton Head to meet the Carolina militia head-on. "If we don't have to stop every time somebody has to go to the bathroom, we could be in the Hilton Head area in three to four days," Governor Stratsworth said.

Meanwhile, Secretary of State George Schultz has already landed in Hilton Head and announced that he is prepared to "stay as long as necessary" to help mediate the dispute. Told at a ninth-hole briefing that rumors were flying that the Carolina militiamen were feeding some of the yankee inhabitants to the many alligators that live on the island, Schultz quipped, "I thought they only ate grits."

Not long ago I was strolling down New York's Fifth Avenue with a native. He pointed out things I'd never thought to observe before.

"Watch the Japanese tourists," he said. "They'll take pictures of anything, even the sky."

That made sense to me. I explained to the New Yorker that in most other parts of the world the sky is blue, and that the visitors from the East probably were intrigued by the fact that the sky in New York has a brownish or yellowish tint to it.

Then my guide told me how to distinguish a native New Yorker from a tourist. "Watch their eyes," he said. "New Yorkers never look up. They either look down or straight ahead. Only visitors to the city look up."

In addition to being bored with tall buildings, I suspected that most natives had suffered some misfortunes with pigeons and therefore did not look up.

My friend further explained that if I watched closely, I would observe that three out of every five New Yorkers would be wearing headsets. "It's our way of dealing with noise pollution," he said.

But if their ears are plugged with loud music, how are they going to hear the two-second blast of the horn which taxi drivers politely give before driving over pedestrians?

Further down Fifth Avenue, my guide showed me yet another point of interest. Along the sidewalk, a crowd gathered to watch large amounts of money changing hands in a little card game being played on top of cardboard boxes. It was like the old shell game: three cards face down, two black and one red. The dealer switches the cards around; the object is to find the red one. I saw people betting as much as a hundred dollars.

"Don't get involved," said the native, "The people you see winning are shills for the dealer. The tourists see them win and so they give it a try, but they almost always lose."

"Isn't that illegal?" I asked.

"Of course, it is," said the native, "but they have lookouts for the police. If a cop heads their way, they simply grab the box and go to another street."

"You said tourists almost always lose. Does that mean some occasionally win?"

"Yes and no," he answered. "If they do happen to win, one of the shills follows them down the street, mugs them and gets the money back."

About that time we passed a group of Japanese tourists. I nodded and said hello to them. They all took my picture as if I were unusual.

They told me about Old Faithful, the world-famous geyser that's the main attraction at Yellowstone National Park in Wyoming, when I was a kid in school. I wasn't much impressed. So every hour on the hour this hole in the ground spews out a lot of steam and hot water. That's a big deal?

Rock City and Disneyland certainly were on my list of things to see when I could afford it, but Old Faithful wasn't in the running. My traveling companion through the wilds of Wyoming, however, had a different idea.

"People come from all over the world to see it," he explained. "We're crazy to come this far and not get a look at it."

I checked the map. We were 120 miles round-trip from Yellowstone. "You want to drive that far just to see hot water and steam?" I asked. "Why don't you just turn on the shower and close the bathroom door tonight?"

He responded by questioning my patriotism, so the next thing I knew we were on our way to Yellowstone, where bears eat people, to see Old Faithful. We arrived just after eight o'clock.

My friend explained that since a major earthquake in the area in 1983, Old Faithful—which previously had been spewing forth on the hour for more than a hundred years—was running as much as eighty-two minutes between eruptions.

"You mean we've come this far and the thing might not even go off?" I complained.

"It'll go off," he said. "That's why they call it Old Faithful."

There must have been three thousand people sitting on benches patiently waiting for the show. Me, I went for an ice cream cone.

"You might miss it," warned my friend.

"So I'll see the highlight film," I quipped.

When I came back with my cone, Old Faithful was smoking a little steam but nothing more. The crowd still waited quietly. Then, at about half past eight, it happened. There was steam, and more steam, and then there was a roar and I think the ground trembled. Old Faithful belched forth with a boiling, steamy column of water that reached over a hundred yards into the sky.

The crowd gasped in awe. The explosion seemed to go higher and higher, and when it ended a few minutes later, the crowd fell silent for a moment before bursting into spontaneous applause.

Later, as we were driving in the darkness of the park, my friend asked me how I felt when I saw Old Faithful come through for her audience.

"Proud to be an American," I answered.

I can't explain why. You just had to be there.

From New York to Dallas, from Florence to Yosemite, there are men, women and children walking around with hearts full of true grit. It may be hidden beneath the surface of poverty, or tattoos, or behind the face of wrinkles, but it's there just the same, pure and clear.

So what if they might be riding Shetland ponies instead of gallant steeds? They all could have ridden alongside Marshall Rooster Cogburn, hallowed be his name and theirs.